INSIDE POETRY

JAMES REEVES
& MARTIN SEYMOUR–SMITH

Inside Poetry

HEINEMANN

LONDON

Heinemann Educational Books Ltd

LONDON   EDINBURGH   MELBOURNE   TORONTO
SINGAPORE   JOHANNESBURG   AUCKLAND
IBADAN   HONG KONG   NAIROBI   NEW DELHI

ISBN 0 435 18771 6 (cased)
ISBN 0 435 18772 4 (paperback)

© JAMES REEVES & MARTIN SEYMOUR-SMITH 1970
First published 1970

Published by
Heinemann Educational Books Ltd
48 Charles Street, London W1X 8AH
Printed by Butler and Tanner Ltd
Frome and London

Contents

vi CONTENTS

Introduction

This book is designed to help students to understand poetry.* By 'understand' we mean in the wider sense, to read, to enjoy and criticize. We offer a wide selection of short poems in English and our selection is divided into three parts. In Part I we offer our own critical appreciations of twenty-five poems, but no supplementary study is suggested in the form of a questionnaire. In Part II we give little commentary of our own but instead a series of suggestions for further study, including many specific questions to indicate the lines of approach we think appropriate for each of twenty-four poems. In Part III we give a further selection of poems for the student to study and write about in his own way, without guidance from us.

We would regard our approach to the practical criticism of poetry as a synthesis of the several critical methods now in use and to some extent in competition. It is no part of our purpose to umpire the conflict between 'appreciation' in the old sense and 'close criticism' or exegesis, called in its purest form 'the new criticism'. We think that both methods have value. Appreciation has the value of subjectivity and of assuming that poetry is to be enjoyed. We regard the reader's personal reaction as valuable— the more so the more it is trained and informed. We regard the objectivity and closeness of intensive criticism as of value in correcting sloppiness of response and in insisting on concentrated attention to the text of a poem. Where, however, this method requires the elimination of subjective response and of knowledge extraneous to the text as it appears on the printed page, we consider it harmful and limiting, and ultimately sterile. The more we know of our own minds and the minds and lives of the poets, the

* It aims to supplement *Understanding Poetry* by James Reeves (Heinemann, 1967), by offering practical work. Although a preliminary reading of the latter will be found helpful, the two books are independent of each other. *Understanding Poetry* will give the wider theoretical basis we have no space for here.

more we shall understand poetry. No relevant information—biographical, psychological, historical, linguistic or whatever—is without use. The important word of course is 'relevant'. The approach we want to inculcate is indicated by our title. We aim at helping students to see poetry from the inside: to get inside the poet and his poem and find out what makes them as they are. Poem and poet interact. They are a continuum. If a poet consciously attempts to break it by writing and living in two compartments, his subconscious will assert itself, and the poem may be other than it might appear to the eyes of the 'objective' critic when he reads it on the printed page. There is also the critic's own unconscious self to be reckoned with. His own tastes and preferences, passions and inhibitions will condition his judgement. It is right they should do so, for criticism written by one who has no personal tastes, preferences, passions and inhibitions is sterile.

We would therefore enjoin the student to give his own feelings and preferences free rein and not to try to write of poems impersonally, as if in fear of an invisible mentor looking over his shoulder. We would stress that our accounts of poems given in Part I are those of two readers and no more. The student is encouraged to differ from us wherever he feels he is right, and so long as he can adduce reasons satisfying to himself. A poem is one of the most complicated organisms to emerge from human creation, and it is not to be expected that any one or two writers can be right about it all the time. To evoke differences of reaction may well be a sign of life and vigour in a poem.

When the reader comes to Part II, it is even more necessary to insist on this. While in many instances there are right answers to our question—answers about which few well-read critics would disagree—there are many questions with open answers. The thoughtful student's answer is as valid as anyone else's. If we sometimes provoke violent disagreement, the book will be on its way to achieving some measure of success.

Our method of questioning in the examples in Part II is an indication of the way in which we think readers should try to get inside poetry. On the whole the simpler questions come first, requiring little more than an intensive concentration on the text.

They are designed to test attentive reading. We move from there to wider questions concerning the poet's technical achievement in prosodic effectiveness and his command of language. In this way the poem is gradually rebuilt in the reader's mind, as from the inside. Lastly we invite comments on the wider questions which will inevitably arise in an active and alert mind after reading a poem. Our counsel to the student would be: 'First, shut out of your mind everything that is not on the printed page. Then, when you have mastered the poet's meaning, consider his methods and how far they help him in conveying his meaning. Finally, open your mind to all those impressions and ideas, more closely or less closely related to the text on the page, which come into it. In this way poetry will come to be integrated into your own life, not simply something external to yourself, an object for abstract and depersonalized dissection.'

Our choice of poems in the three parts of this book has been dictated partly by a belief in the interest and in some cases the worth of the poems, partly by their susceptibility to questions and analysis, and partly by a wish to offer a representative choice of short poems from the whole range of English and American poetry, from Chaucer to the present. The book is not, however, an anthology. If any student considers that there are 'gaps' in our selection, he is invited to fill them himself when he comes to work on Part III, in which the poems are arranged alphabetically.

Acknowledgements

The authors and publisher wish to thank the following for permission to reproduce copyright material: The trustees of the Hardy Estate and Macmillan & Co. Ltd for 'Last Words to a Dumb Friend', 'Friends Beyond' and 'Ah, are you digging on my grave' by Thomas Hardy from *The Collected Poems*; John Crowe Ransom and Eyre & Spottiswoode Ltd for 'Necrological' from *Selected Poems*; Oxford University Press Inc. (New York) for 'The Nameless Ones' by Conrad Aiken from *Collected Poems*; Macmillan Co. Inc. for 'Flammonde' by Edwin Arlington Robinson from *The Man Against the Sky*; The Society of Authors as the literary representative of the Estate of A. E. Housman and Jonathan Cape Ltd for 'The night is freezing fast' from *Collected Poems*; Mr Harold Owen and Chatto & Windus Ltd for 'Dulce et Decorum Est' from *The Collected Poems of Wilfred Owen*; Anthony Conran and Penguin Books Ltd for 'Llywarch the Old'; Kenneth Ashley and The Bodley Head for 'Goods Train at Night' from *Up Hill and Down Dale*; J. M. Russell and Routledge and Kegan Paul Ltd for 'Burma II'; Henry Reed and Jonathan Cape Ltd for 'Outside and In' from *A Map of Verona*; Holt Rinehart and Winston Inc. and Jonathan Cape Ltd for 'Mending Wall' by Robert Frost from *The Complete Poems of Robert Frost*; A. D. Peters and Co. for 'Report on Experience' and 'The Ballast-Hole' by Edmund Blunden; The Literary Trustees of Walter de la Mare and the Society of Authors as their representative for 'The Children of Stare' and 'The Railway Junction'; Faber and Faber Ltd for 'Suburban Dream' by Edwin Muir from *Collected Poems 1921–1958*, for 'Egypt' by Keith Douglas from *Collected Poems*, and for 'Dance of the Macabre Mice' and 'The Emperor of Ice-Cream' by Wallace Stevens from *Collected Poems*.

Part I

Part I

I. HARTLEY COLERIDGE: *'Tis strange to me . . .*

> 'Tis strange to me, who long have seen no face
> That was not like a book whose every page
> I knew by heart, a kindly common-place—
> And faithful record of progressive age—
> To wander forth and view an unknown race;   5
> Of all that I have been to find no trace,
> No footstep of my by-gone pilgrimage.
> Thousands I pass, and no one stays his pace
> To tell me that the day is fair, or rainy—
> Each one his object seeks with anxious chase,   10
> And I have not a common hope with any—
> Thus like one drop of oil upon a flood,
> In uncommunicating solitude—
> Single am I amongst the countless many.

The writer of this poem expresses, in a direct but controlled way, his sense of loneliness, of isolation, or, as it is now called, alienation. He has lived for a long time among familiar faces: we know it is a long time because he mentions the 'record of progressive age'. He now finds himself in a new atmosphere: line 8 makes it clear that he is in a town, whereas before, it is reasonable to assume, he was in the country. He feels cut off from his roots and, 'like one drop of oil upon a flood', he is almost of another 'race', a different species. All are hurrying about their appointed tasks and have no communication with the writer.

Alienation is sometimes written of as if it were a new phenomenon. It has been felt perhaps for as long as man has existed, and poets have written of it, relieving the loneliness by realizing it in poetic form. Hartley Coleridge's sonnet is neither sentimental nor overladen with self-pity. He states his situation in an almost matter-of-fact way, neither dramatizing it nor pouring out buckets of tears in the manner of his contemporary Byron. There is a quiet manliness about his tone which commends itself to the most reticent and least hysterical reader.

The effectiveness of this poem is due in part to the technical control by which, under the appearance of a natural artlessness and simplicity, Hartley Coleridge manages the sonnet form. It is not easy to write in this form without either forcing the syntax and the vocabulary to fit the rhyme-scheme or padding out the thought with repetition in order to make it fit the fourteen-line mould. It would be difficult to convict Hartley Coleridge of either fault. He was, indeed, a master of the form, and most of his best poems are sonnets. The advantage of the form is that a poet is obliged to control his emotion, so that, paradoxically, the very artificiality of the form makes directness and sincerity easier to achieve. Coleridge's liking for the sonnet is partly temperamental: by contrast, it is impossible to imagine, say, D. H. Lawrence, author of *Pansies* and other very direct examples of free verse, having the patience and the craftsmanlike control of emotion to achieve a good sonnet. This is not to disparage Lawrence's poetry: it is simply to point out that one of the marks of a true poet is that he can discover the form which suits his unique temperament and gifts.

In the kind of unrhetorical, natural poem which Coleridge tries to write, even in as strict a form as the sonnet, one of the aims must be to avoid inversions of the prose order of words for the sake of rhyme or rhythm. Such inversions, if they occur, should be justifiable on grounds of poetic effect. After all, even in ordinary prose conversation we sometimes invert the normal English word-order to secure emphasis: 'Never have I heard such a noise!' 'I don't mind cats, but dogs I can't abide.' In this sonnet there are four inversions: line 6 runs, 'Of all that I have been to find no trace'. To have used the prose order ('To find no trace of all that I have been') would have upset the rhyme-pattern. But the inversion can be justified on the ground of emphasis: 'no trace' is stronger coming at the end of the line. The same justification may be made for the opening of line 8, 'Thousands I pass', where the word 'Thousands' is stressed, coming first. Moreover, the relapse to a natural order and lowering of tone in the next line ('To tell me that the day is fair, or rainy'), by contrast with line 8, has an effect of simple pathos. The next line ('Each one his object seeks with anxious chase') is perhaps the most awkward in the poem. There is a touch here of the artificial style of the late

eighteenth century, a touch of elegant tautology in the juxta-
position of 'seeks' and 'chase'. But from now on the word-order
is that of prose speech until the very last line ('Single am I
amongst the countless many'), which, with its emphasis on
'Single', and the opposition of 'Single' to 'many' (taking up the
theme of the drop of oil on the flood), sums up the whole poem
and clinches the thought.

A glance at the line-endings will show that only four rhymes
are used throughout, and these with a high degree of point and
naturalness. The sonnet achieves its effectiveness with very little
use of figurative language. Indeed, the book simile beginning in
line 2 and the 'drop of oil' simile in line 12 are the only real figures
in the poem, and they are crucial. In the main the generally intel-
lectual tone of the poem, dignified and restrained, derives from
the use of such expressions as 'faithful record of progressive age',
'a common hope' and 'uncommunicating solitude'.

2. EMILY DICKINSON: *There's been a death . . .*

There's been a death in the opposite house
As lately as today.
I know it by the numb look
Such houses have alway.

The neighbours rustle in and out;   5
The doctor drives away.
A window opens like a pod,
Abrupt, mechanically;

Somebody flings a mattress out.
The children hurry by;   10
They wonder if it died on that.
I used to, when a boy.

The minister goes stiffly in
As if the house were his
And he owned all the mourners now,   15
And little boys besides;

And then the milliner, and the man
Of the appalling trade
To take the measure of the house.
There'll be that dark parade   20

Of tassels and of coaches soon.
It's easy as a sign—
The intuition of the news
In just a country town.

Emily Dickinson was an American poet who lived from 1830
until 1886. She spent nearly all her life in Amherst, Massachusetts,
where her father was a lawyer. She was a gay and lively girl, but
as she grew older she tended to become more and more of a
recluse. Less than a dozen of her poems were published in her
lifetime, during which they were a closely-guarded secret.

According to T. S. Eliot, the Elizabethan poet and dramatist Webster 'was much possessed by death'. This is equally true of Emily Dickinson. She was possessed by the thought of death because she was intensely alive and in love with life. But living as she did an increasingly solitary life, she dwelt much on the basic truths of life and death and the after-life in which, as a conforming Christian, she believed. As a poet, however, she was fascinated by the paradox that, in order to achieve immortality in Heaven, it was necessary to undergo the complete cessation, the abrupt termination of all that life meant, all that human consciousness contained. This poem on a funeral, probably in her native town of Amherst, Massachusetts, is a graphic evocation of an experience that clearly affected her deeply, since a death always called into question the very foundations of her whole attitude to life.

Her account of the death is the reverse of morbid. She dwells, not on the dead person (we are not told even if it is a man, a woman or a child) but on the effect of the death on the small community. In the brief twenty-four lines four essential individuals are mentioned (doctor, milliner, undertaker and minister) as well as an anonymous 'somebody' who throws a mattress out of the window and a chorus of 'neighbours', 'children' and 'little boys'. Only the protagonist in this Greek drama in miniature is kept off the stage. The comparison with Greek drama is strengthened by an example of the Greek practice of referring to something which causes fear or displeasure by a euphemism: 'the man / Of the appalling trade' and 'the house' in stanza 5 are, of course, the undertaker and the coffin.

The starkness of Emily Dickinson's experience of the occurrence is conveyed by the bareness and economy of the diction. Epithets are used sparingly, and this gives the greater point to such words as 'numb' in line 3 and 'dark' in line 20. Another example of the indirectness of approach mentioned earlier is in stanza 3: 'They wonder if *it* died on *that*' (our italics). The depersonalization of the dead gives a *frisson* to our reaction. Emily Dickinson, when speaking of herself as a child, usually refers to herself as 'a boy'. It is no part of her intention to insist on her femininity as a poet.

It would be hard to discover a superfluous word in the poem or an inversion of the word-order of common speech. If we looked for perfect rhymes in an *abcb* pattern, we might say that rhyme has been sacrificed to word-order. In stanza 2 'away' is paired with 'mechanically', and in stanza 3 'by' with 'boy'. Only in 1 and 5 are full rhymes used. Yet these half-rhymes or assonances may be justified on the ground that in such regularly metrical, even conventionally constructed stanzas, full rhymes throughout might give the appearance of monotony. The assonances help to preserve the freshness, the spontaneity of utterance which is one of Emily Dickinson's most outstanding qualities.

Another feature of this poem, as of many by the same author, is its coolness of tone. Death is the most obvious subject about which to become rhetorical, to overstate.

> Death that hath sucked the honey of thy breath
> Hath had no power yet upon thy beauty.

Romeo's apostrophe to the apparently dead Juliet is magnificent, but it is drama. It is rhetoric. Coolness of tone would have been out of place, even bathetic. Emily Dickinson has no use for rhetoric. Instead, she aims at control, a detached and objective viewing of the event. Such expressions as the remarkable simile 'like a pod' and 'the intuition of the news' contribute to this effect. There is thus a balance between spontaneity and control, and this is one of the mysteries of all really good poetry. Does the poet's emotion (a kind of tight suspense, a fearful fascination) control her, or does she control it?

There is an almost Greek inevitability in the progress of the dead 'it' from 'the opposite house', which is part of a bustling and busy neighbourhood, to the final solitary 'house' to be constructed by the 'appalling' undertaker (who was probably himself the carpenter). The surface simplicity and apparent artlessness of the poem conceal depths of suggestion and complexity.

3. JOHN CLARE: *Country Letter*

Dear brother Robin, this comes from us all
With our kind love, and could Gip write and all
Though but a dog he'd have his love to spare,
For still he knows, and by your corner chair
The moment he comes in he lies him down   5
And seems to fancy you are in the town.
This leaves us well in health, thank God for that!
For old acquaintance Sue has kept your hat
Which mother brushes ere she lays it by
And every Sunday goes upstairs to cry.   10
Jane still is yours till you come back agen
And ne'er so much as dances with the men;
And Ned the woodman every week comes in
And asks about you kindly as our kin;
And he with this and goody Thompson sends   15
Remembrances with those of all our friends.
Father with us sends love until he hears
And mother she has nothing but her tears,
Yet wishes you like us in health the same
And longs to see a letter with your name,   20
So, loving brother, don't forget to write.
Old Gip lies on the hearth stone every night;
Mother can't bear to turn him out of doors
And never noises now of dirty floors;
Father will laugh but lets her have her way,   25
And Gip for kindness get a double pay.
So Robin write and let us quickly see
You don't forget old friends no more than we,
Nor let my mother have so much to blame
To go three journeys ere your letter came.   30

John Clare, an agricultural labourer, was born and bred in
Northamptonshire at a difficult time for farmers. He early dis-
covered an inborn love of poetry and nothing could stop him
from writing poems of his own. Although highly intelligent, he
was more or less self-educated—a handicap that ruined his life.

He never lost his love of country life and the ways in which he had been brought up, but his initial success as a poet alienated him from the people of his neighbourhood. He knew that poems were written for, and read by, sophisticated readers in London and the towns. Yet he seldom wrote patronizingly and, except for a few lapses—verses of the 'keepsake' variety and 'imitations' of other poets—he always wrote truthfully and, in the deepest sense, passionately about the things and people he knew and understood.

In *Country Letter* he composes a fictional letter to a 'brother Robin', who has left the village and gone far away—whether temporarily or permanently we are not told. It is immaterial. The poem is about two things—Robin's absence and the feelings of those who miss him. The first success of the poem is what we should call a technical one, though it is questionable if Clare himself would have thought he was creating a technical triumph. The poem is in all details in the language of country speech, yet it is in rhymed iambic pentameters. The verse technique is unobtrusive, indeed, unexciting: it is not meant to be exciting. One can almost imagine that country people at the close of the eighteenth century spoke in pentameters. There are no inversions of natural speech-order and no literary devices. The whole poem is plain to the point of bareness.

This plainness is the mark of Clare's natural taste and feeling. He could write poems in a more artificial and literary style, with more rhetoric and heightening of tone: but in *Country Letter* he knows instinctively that all artifice would be out of place and instantly destroy the illusion: that is, the illusion that we are reading a personal letter from a young countryman to his absent brother.

In a mere fifteen couplets we are given what is almost a simple drama, a representation of the domestic life of a group disrupted by the absence of one of its members. First, we are told of the distress of the dog Gip. This is a remarkable touch of realism, for domestic animals are always the first and most obvious sufferers from such a disturbance of the accepted order. The dog, in fact, almost steals the poem, not only on account of its own distress but because it is accorded special treatment. Next we hear of Sue, presumably a sister, who, together with Mother, pays special attention to the hat Robin has left behind, a sort of talisman or token of the departed one. Then we hear of Mother, who cries each Sunday for her son. Some may think that the mention of Mother's tears brings the poem near to the verge of sentimentality. We do not think so, for there is a thin dividing-line between sentiment and sentimentality, the observance of which is the mark of a true poet. However, the mood changes with the mention of Jane, the sweetheart, who, in fidelity to her absent lover, 'ne'er so much as dances with' other men. Then the neighbours, Ned the woodman and Goody Thompson, enquire solicitously about Robin's welfare and send greetings. Lastly, Father is mentioned in a somewhat reserved vein—'love until he hears'. This is the first mention of the fact that Robin is a bad correspondent and has evidently not kept his promise to write. Indeed, it is Robin's failure to communicate that is the cause of the family's distress and the occasion for the letter. It is clear that a letter among these people is no commonplace matter. Letters were not delivered to remote villages by postmen; it was necessary to go to town and collect them, and the fact that Mother has to go to town three times before she gets a letter is a source of concern and grief. There is even perhaps a hint of anxiety as to whether some ill has befallen the absent son. As if to balance the sentiment, the simple warmth of the letter, there is a strong note of reproof in the tone of the writer as he orders Robin to be a more regular correspondent. Yet nothing is overstated or dramatized.

Sophisticated readers are still inclined to treat Clare as a 'natural', an artless 'peasant poet' (which is how his first publisher announced him), yet the feeling of this poem, as of so many others, classes him as what can only be called a natural aristocrat —using the word in its true sense of 'one of the best'. If it is thought that this kind of poem is easy to write, that it demands no skill or technique, one can only ask, 'Where else in English poetry is anything quite like it to be found?' Certainly few, if any, literary writers—educated at universities—could have achieved these thirty lines without at some point betraying their background. Other writers have written in the supposed persons of simple countrymen, but they commonly give themselves away by a note of exaggeration or parody. There is not a word of either in *Country Letter*. There is no note of the *faux-naif* common in the usual 'rustic' style. It tends to make some radio scripts about 'rural' characters, effective though they may be in their popular way, seem contrived.

4. TERENCE HARDS: *Hansey*

Poor Hansey, lank dissembler,
Concealed throughout the vital key
To his lugubrious anxiety,
Which was that he abhorred a middle course
Yet was not qualified for harsh extremes.   5

Thus, married in default of prudence,
Though prudence might prompt other men to wed,
He soon found seven children to be fed
And knew that violence must be done
To either private principles or public conscience.   10

He should not now refuse to work,
Go drinking, loafing, give his cash away
Nor write a book and let his teeth decay,
Yet would not paint the house, have hobbies,
Shave or show an interest in his job.   15

So Hansey, hating compromise
But neither able to make reckless bets
Nor to meticulously pay his debts,
Died at last with unattended teeth—
Though in a hospital and well insured.   20

Hansey, presumably a nickname ('Hans' in Dutch and German
is short for 'John', suggesting in English an everyday man who
might be anyone; it also strikes a somewhat self-mocking note),
is 'lugubrious' because his nature forces him to be a 'dissembler'
—one who hides the essential 'key' to his problem. The problem
he has to live with is that he despises compromise, a 'middle
course' between conventionality on the one hand and the bohe-
mian attitude. If he were 'qualified' for what he feels is the bohe-
mian life of a committed writer, things would be simpler. They
would also be simpler if he had no ambition beyond a life of
domesticity—earning a livelihood for himself, his wife and his
seven children, helping in the house, getting his teeth seen to

by regular visits to the dentist. He married imprudently, and what he calls 'public conscience'—a conventional regard for what the neighbours would say—compels him to earn his livelihood by a regular job, while 'private conscience' urges him to a more unconventional course. Stanza 3 points to his dilemma and emphasizes the necessity for a life of compromise. Thus Hansey ends his days with neglected teeth but in a hospital, leaving a life insurance policy behind, just like any ordinary husband, to take care of his family.

This is the mere prose paraphrase of a compressed and graphic account, in twenty lines, of a man's life. There can be little doubt that the poet is writing of himself, but objectively, as if to distance himself from his own predicament and see it in the context of common humanity. The tone is ironical: there is no rhetoric or self-pitying parade of a sense of guilt or frustration. The facts are faced squarely and sardonically, tragic as they may be. There is no Byronic posturing in an attempt to elevate a chosen individual above the common run of men. To be sure, the poem starts with the epithet 'poor', but that is the only hint of self-pity. No doubt *Hansey* is a picture of a situation experienced by many men. The difference between Hansey and the ordinary run of those who conform to conventional ways and standards is that Hansey remains lugubriously anxious about himself. His nature does not allow him to enjoy a commonplace suburban existence; he can only regard the other kind of life with wistful regret and stoicism.

It should perhaps be pointed out that the 'unconventionality' of writers does not necessarily consist of bohemianism, or of not paying debts or allowing the teeth to rot. A writer may or may not be bohemian, although many writers—owing to the exigencies of the profession—have seemed to be so. But what is important is a writer's truth to his own nature and view of things—as admirably exemplified in this poem.

The poem achieves its effect by a masterly and unobtrusive compression and economy. It proceeds, not by a full enumeration of details, but by a kind of shorthand. We are meant to supply the details of the life of a man whose rejection of conventional values is instanced by a refusal to have his teeth seen to and to help with interior decoration or to go in for 'hobbies'. Other men might solace themselves with photography or golf. Hansey refuses to do this because he sees himself as one who, better qualified, might write a book. There is a hint that, even after marriage and the arrival of seven mouths to feed, he drinks, loafs and indulges a generosity he cannot afford. The ironic conclusion is that the hater of compromise ends in a compromise death. There is not a superfluous word or phrase in these twenty lines, which indeed, are a model of one kind of contemporary poetry —the kind which shuns affectation, obscurity and verbosity and is in reaction against the verbosity of Victorians such as Browning. Terence Hards is a poet who at his best knows how to begin, to develop and to end a poem—he knows where and how to stop. He knows how to give each phrase its maximum effect. It might be said that this is a dry, unromantic poem; but that does not mean that it is without feeling. Indeed it is full of humanity and honest self-analysis. It is the reverse of exhibitionistic, and remains pointed and memorable when more showy pieces have faded in the reader's mind.

5. WILLIAM WORDSWORTH: *Extempore Effusion upon the Death of James Hogg*

When first descending from the moorlands
I saw the Stream of Yarrow glide
Along a bare and open valley,
The Ettrick Shepherd was my guide.

When last along its banks I wandered,   5
Through groves that had begun to shed
Their golden leaves upon the pathway,
My steps the Border-minstrel led.

The mighty Minstrel breathes no longer,
'Mid mouldering ruins low he lies;   10
And death upon the braes of Yarrow,
Has closed the Shepherd-poet's eyes.

Nor has the rolling year twice measured,
From sign to sign, its steadfast course,
Since every mortal power of Coleridge   15
Was frozen at its marvellous source;

The rapt One, of the godlike forehead,
The heaven-eyed creature sleeps in earth:
And Lamb, the frolic and the gentle,
Has vanished from his lonely hearth.   20

Like clouds that rake the mountain-summits,
Or waves that own no curbing hand,
How fast has brother followed brother,
From sunshine to the sunless land!

Yet I, whose lids from infant slumber   25
Were earlier raised, remain to hear
A timid voice, that asks in whispers,
'Who next will drop and disappear?'

Our haughty life is crowned with darkness,
Like London with its own black wreath,   30
On which with thee, O Crabbe! forth-looking,
I gazed from Hampstead's breezy heath.

As if but yesterday departed,
Thou too art gone before; but why,
O'er ripe fruit, seasonably gathered,   35
Should frail survivors heave a sigh?

Mourn rather for that holy Spirit,
Sweet as the spring, as ocean deep,
For Her who, ere her summer faded,
Has sunk into a breathless sleep.   40

No more of old romantic sorrows,
For slaughtered Youth or love-lorn Maid!
With sharper grief is Yarrow smitten,
And Ettrick mourns with her their Poet dead.

Wordsworth wrote this poem in 1835, after reading about the death of James Hogg in a newspaper. For almost thirty years (since 1807 or 1808) he had written little poetry of any account. This is almost universally agreed upon, and attempts to demonstrate otherwise have been conspicuous failures. This poem, then, represents an oasis in a desert of mediocrity; for if the later Wordsworth was never the reprehensible political apostate he was once taken to be, he was nevertheless a singularly poor poet and a monstrous egoist. In writing this poem, he was deeply moved—as the title indicates, he composed it much more quickly, and under greater pressure of emotion, than was his wont.

He laments the death of six friends who were also poets: Hogg (died 1835), called the Ettrick Shepherd, author of *Confessions of a Justified Sinner* and a book of clever parodies of contemporary poets (including Wordsworth), *The Poetic Mirror*; Scott (died 1832); Coleridge (died 1834); Lamb (died 1834); Crabbe (died 1832); and, rather incongruously, Felicia Hemans, 'that holy Spirit', authoress of *Casabianca*, who died in 1835.

Wordsworth had not got on at all well with Hogg, had had a serious quarrel with Coleridge (eventually patched up, but only nominally) and was too egotistic ever to enthuse much over the poetry of any of his living contemporaries. But reading of the death of Hogg suddenly awakened worthier emotions—the ones that characterized the man who wrote the best of his poems.

Fundamentally, despite the pose of cautious optimism and official Christian hope he put on in middle and old age, Wordsworth was a gloomy and pessimistic man. This poem aptly demonstrates the kind of real serenity—sad, though dignified—of which he was capable.

The poem itself is extremely direct, and requires little explanation. It is interesting to consider how it achieves its power. First and foremost, of course, it is a moving poem because the author himself was deeply moved when he wrote it. Moreover, his feelings are dignified and expressed without cliché. In solemn iambic verse, he makes a series of simple statements. The description of the valley in line 3, 'bare and open', establishes the austere mood. Note also the elegiac cadence of the feminine endings (lines 3, 5, 7, 9). In the fourth and fifth stanzas all Wordsworth's true feeling, admiration for and gratitude to Coleridge, which he had seldom expressed or acted on, emerge: he pays tribute to his 'marvellous' powers—when he first heard of Coleridge's death he had used a similar word, saying that he had been the most 'wonderful' man he had ever known—and to his 'godlike' intellect. Then comes the tribute to Lamb, containing the happy phrase, 'the frolic and the gentle'.

In stanza 7 he frankly faces the fact of his own eventual death. Indeed, primitive fear of death, now that he is sixty-five, provides part at least of the motive behind this generous elegy. The passage beginning with the first line of the eighth stanza, 'Our haughty life is crowned with darkness', sums up Wordsworth's attitude to life. It is an attitude of sadness and regret; and yet it affirms the existence of beauty. Although it is a poem that mourns the passing of six people, it contains no suggestion that the poet believes in any Christian kind of immortality. It tends to confirm the general belief that the Christian piety of Wordsworth's later days was fundamentally insincere—or, if that is too strong a word, then let us say that it was a matter of self-deception.

However, there is plenty of proudly non-Christian energy and dignity in this final bright flicker of poetry from one who had long ago turned fearfully from the exciting dangers of poetry to the turgid gratifications of preaching in verse.

6. ROBERT FROST: *Mending Wall*

Something there is that doesn't love a wall,
That sends the frozen-ground-swell under it,
And spills the upper boulders in the sun;
And makes gaps even two can pass abreast.
The work of hunters is another thing: 5
I have come after them and made repair
Where they have left not one stone on a stone,
But they would have the rabbit out of hiding,
To please the yelping dogs. The gaps I mean,
No one has seen them made or heard them made,   10
But at spring mending-time we find them there.
I let my neighbour know beyond the hill;
And on a day we meet to walk the line
And set the wall between us once again.
We keep the wall between us as we go.   15
To each the boulders that have fallen to each.
And some are loaves and some so nearly balls
We have to use a spell to make them balance:
'Stay where you are until our backs are turned!'
We wear our fingers rough with handling them.   20
Oh, just another kind of outdoor game,
One on a side. It comes to little more:
There where it is we do not need the wall:
He is all pine and I am apple orchard.
My apple trees will never get across   25
And eat the cones under his pines, I tell him.
He only says, 'Good fences make good neighbours.'
Spring is the mischief in me, and I wonder
If I could put a notion in his head:
'*Why* do they make good neighbours? Isn't it   30
Where there are cows? But here there are no cows.
Before I built a wall I'd ask to know
What I was walling in or walling out,
And to whom I was like to give offence.
Something there is that doesn't love a wall,   35
That wants it down.' I could say 'Elves' to him,
But it's not elves exactly, and I'd rather

He said it for himself. I see him there
Bringing a stone grasped firmly by the top
In each hand, like an old-stone savage armed.   40
He moves in darkness as it seems to me,
Not of woods only and the shade of trees.
He will not go behind his father's saying,
And he likes having thought of it so well
He says again, 'Good fences make good neighbours.'   45

Frost is here developing an idea which has come to him during
the annual process of meeting his farming neighbour to repair
the damage to their boundary wall which has occurred during
the winter months. Almost exactly the first half of the poem is
straightforward narrative or description. The two neighbours
meet and move along on opposite sides of the wall, replacing the
stones that have fallen on one side or the other. The narrative is
in the present tense, which gives the impression that Frost is
ruminating, as the 'game', as he calls it, proceeds. Then at line
23 a change occurs. Frost begins to think about the implications
of this annual spring ritual. 'There where it is, we do not need
the wall.' But there is a difference of attitude, of temperament
between the two neighbours. The other man cannot see the
force of Frost's point that pines and apple-trees cannot interfere
with each other if there is no fence between. The neighbour's
attitude, reflecting a rigid and conservative temperament, is
summed up in the proverbial adage, 'Good fences make good
neighbours'. But this is not Frost's idea of neighbourliness, which
to him is something prevented or destroyed by fences. So he
begins to see the neighbour, not just as a man playing an outdoor
game, but as 'an old-stone savage armed' who 'moves in darkness',
the darkness of a primitive and hostile mind acting solely accord-
ing to the customs of ancestral wisdom. 'Something there is that
doesn't love a wall', he repeats ruefully. Frost dismisses the
whimsical notion that it is some supernatural creature, like elves,
that destroys the wall. His neighbour would not appreciate the
suggestion.

The line with which Frost begins the poem, and which he
repeats towards the end, has also something of the force of a

proverb. This is stressed by the fact that, in a poem whose tone and language are natural and homely, it is almost the only line having an inverted word-order. We are asked to pay special attention to that 'Something' that hates walls. What is it? Not hunters, not elves, but of course winter—the 'frost' that gets into the wall and dislodges the stones, the frost that 'sends the frozen-ground-swell . . .' It is impossible to ignore the suggestion of a pun on the poet's name. It is 'Frost' that doesn't love walls. Such an idea would be perfectly in keeping with Frost's occasional impish humour. *Mending Wall* is thus a plea for love between neighbours, for civilized relations, for tolerance and the removal of barriers to communication between men. What began as a straightforward account of an annual operation between two farmers ends as an expression of the need for communication.

But Frost is not preaching. The poem has its message, but this grows out of the narrative in an organic and natural manner, as one thought grows out of another in the mind or in good music. The interest remains in the poet's self-revelation as he ruminates on the operation in progress. That this operation is of paramount interest is underlined by the graphic, concrete and homely language in which the poem is written. It is this style—the voice of an educated yet practical American—that is the hallmark of all Frost's best work. It is never strident, never rhetorical. It gains its effect from under-, not over-statement. It is a speech which seems to have grown out of the soil of America. Yet the very plainness of Frost's style is deceptive. His skill lies in retaining a natural and personal voice, while accommodating the prose rhythm to the structure of the iambic pentameter. Whenever a line is wholly regular (such as 'My apple trees will never get across') it is followed by something irregular ('And eat the cones under his pines, I tell him'). There is no flatness and no monotony. It sounds easy, but it took much learning, much thought and experiment.

7. JONATHAN SWIFT: *A Description of a City Shower*

Careful Observers may fortel the Hour
(By sure Prognosticks) when to dread a Show'r:
While Rain depends, the pensive Cat gives o'er
Her Frolicks, and pursues her Tail no more.
Returning Home at Night, you'll find the Sink   5
Strike your offended Sense with double Stink.
If you be wise, then go not far to Dine,
You'll spend in Coach-hire more than save in Wine.
A coming Show'r your shooting Corns presage,
Old Aches throb, your hollow Tooth will rage.   10
Sauntring in Coffee-house is *Dulman* seen;
He damns the Climate, and complains of Spleen.

Mean while the South rising with dabbled Wings,
A Sable Cloud a-thwart the Welkin flings,
That swill'd more Liquor than it could contain,   15
And like a Drunkard gives it up again.
Brisk *Susan* whips her Linen from the Rope,
While the first drizzling Show'r is born aslope,
Such is that Sprinkling which some careless Quean
Flirts on you from her Mop, but not so clean.   20
You fly, invoke the Gods; then turning, stop
To rail; she singing, still whirls on her Mop.
Not yet, the Dust had shun'd th' unequal Strife,
But aided by the Wind, fought still for Life;
And wafted with its Foe by violent Gust,   25
'Twas doubtful which was Rain, and which was Dust.
Ah! where must needy Poet seek for Aid,
When Dust and Rain at once his Coat invade;
His only Coat, where Dust confus'd with Rain,
Roughen the Nap, and leave a mingled Stain.   30

Now in contiguous Drops the Flood comes down,
Threat'ning with Deluge this *Devoted* Town.
To Shops in Crouds the daggled Females fly,
Pretend to cheapen Goods, but nothing buy.

The Templar spruce, while ev'ry Spout's a-broach,   35
Stays till 'tis fair, yet seems to call a Coach.
The tuck'd-up Sempstress walks with hasty Strides,
While Streams run down her oil'd Umbrella's Sides.
Here various Kinds by various Fortunes led,
Commence Acquaintance underneath a Shed.   40
Triumphant Tories, and desponding Whigs,
Forget their Fewds, and join to save their Wigs,
Box'd in a Chair the Beau impatient sits,
While Spouts run clatt'ring o'er the Roof by Fits;
And ever and anon with frightful Din   45
The Leather sounds, he trembles from within.
So when *Troy* Chair-men bore the Wooden Steed,
Pregnant with *Greeks*, impatient to be freed,
(Those Bully *Greeks*, who, as the Moderns do,
Instead of paying Chair-men, run them thro'.)   50
Laoco'n struck the Outside with his Spear,
And each imprison'd Hero quak'd for Fear.

Now from all Parts the swelling Kennels flow,
And bear their Trophies with them as they go:
Filth of all Hues and Odours seem to tell   55
What Street they sail'd from, by their Sight and Smell.
They, as each Torrent drives, with rapid Force
From *Smithfield*, or St. *Pulchre's* shape their Course,
And in huge *Confluent* join at *Snow-Hill* Ridge,
Fall from the *Conduit* prone to *Holborn-Bridge*,   60
Sweepings from Butchers Stalls, Dung, Guts, and Blood,
Drown'd Puppies, stinking Sprats, all drench'd in Mud,
Dead Cats and Turnip-Tops come tumbling down the Flood.

Swift began, in the last decade of the seventeenth century, by writing poetry in the 'sublime' style that was then fashionable. These poems were unsuccessful, and he soon gave up writing in this way. All his poems from 1698 onwards are in a plain style, which looks back to that of Samuel Butler's *Hudibras*, rather than Dryden's, which most of the Augustan poets—such as Pope—followed.

Dr Johnson, in his life of Swift, said that 'there is not much upon which the critick can exercise his powers'. Perhaps this is why his poetry has attracted so little criticism. Yet F. W. Bateson, one of the editors of the great Twickenham edition of Pope, has stated that Swift was the better poet.

In this poem, written in 1710, Swift is partly poking fun at the sublime style, which was affected by—among others—Joseph Addison, with whom he was then associated. Thus, lines 13 and 14 collapse into the deliberate bathos of line 16 (which recalls *The Tempest*, II, 2, 'yond same black cloud . . . looks like a foul wombat that would shed his liquor'). (Notice also the mock-heroic Homeric simile of lines 47–52.)   Yet here, as in the rest of this surprisingly effective and realistic poem, Swift was doing something more than merely sending up a style that prevailed too long and had become stale; he had only intended to write a piece of urban realism in contrast to the unrealistic pastoral descriptions that were then so fashionable. But he achieved a type of poetry that had never been seen in England before. A plain type of poetry, but one full of possibilities, at a time when much English writing had become trivial and false. In 1710, a city shower would not fashionably have been supposed to be a 'proper' subject for poetry. Hence Swift's choice of it. As Swift's chief editor writes, 'The whole poem is built on scenes and incidents observed.'

In line 2 the word 'dread' gives the clue to Swift's satirical intentions: no one, of course, 'dreads' a shower. But his observations are strikingly accurate and careful. In the stuffy weather before rain comes, cats stop playing, sinks smell, corns and aches (pronounced 'aitches') throb, and dull people feel depressed. Lines 27–30 contain a reference to the proverbial poverty of poets in Swift's time.

The poem is remarkable for the manner in which it contrasts the kind of satire exemplified by the use of the words 'dread' and, in line 32, '*Devoted*' (pious, in the religious sense), with simple description. 'Daggled' means 'bedraggled'; 'cheapen' means 'to bargain for'. The 'Templer spruce' is a well-dressed young law-student who is anxious to conceal the fact that he cannot afford to pay for a coach. 'Kennels' were the gutters that then ran down the centre of the streets. The last triplet is supposed (as Swift himself said) to satirize 'that licentious Manner of modern Poets, in making three Rhimes together'; in fact it is a triumph of descriptive accuracy.

It is an excellent and instructive exercise, for those who are interested in writing poems, to use this as a model for writing a set of rhyming couplets on their own home environment.

8. SAMUEL JOHNSON: *On the Death of Mr Robert Levet a Practiser in Physic*

Condemn'd to hope's delusive mine,
    As on we toil from day to day,
By sudden blasts, or slow decline,
    Our social comforts drop away.

Well tried through many a varying year,   5
    See Levet to the grave descend;
Officious, innocent, sincere,
    Of ev'ry friendless name the friend,

Yet still he fills affection's eye,
    Obscurely wise, and coarsely kind;   10
Nor, letter'd arrogance, deny
    Thy praise to merit unrefin'd.

When fainting nature call'd for aid,
    And hov'ring death prepar'd the blow,
His vig'rous remedy display'd   15
    The power of art without the show.

In misery's darkest caverns known,
    His useful care was ever nigh,
Where hopeless anguish pour'd his groan,
    And lonely want retir'd to die.   20

No summons mock'd by chill delay,
    No petty gain disdain'd by pride,
The modest wants of ev'ry day
    The toil of ev'ry day supplied.

His virtues walk'd their narrow round,   25
    Nor made a pause, nor left a void;
And sure th' Eternal Master found
    The single talent well employ'd.

The busy day, the peaceful night,
    Unfelt, uncounted, glided by;   30

His frame was firm, his powers were bright,
   Tho' now his eightieth year was nigh.

Then with no fiery throbbing pain,
   No cold gradations of decay,
Death broke at once the vital chain,   35
   And free'd his soul the nearest way.

Robert Levet was one of Dr Johnson's pensioners and for many
years had served as surgeon to his household. He died in 1782
at the age of seventy-six. Two months later Johnson recited this
poem to Boswell with great feeling. He was always deeply dis-
turbed by death and terrified, almost to the point of morbidity,
at the thought of it. He was also always distressed by the loss
of a friend. Indeed, his pleasure in friendship—one of his dearest
pleasures—was always qualified by the thought that it could and
must end. 'Friendship between mortals,' he wrote in *The Rambler*,
'can be contracted on no other terms than that one must some
time mourn for the other's death.' So Johnson begins his tribute
to the dead friend by lamenting that the 'social comforts' of life
gradually disappear. The neat and weighty phrase of the first line
is also characteristic. The 'mine' (presumably one for gold or
jewels) to which we are condemned is a metaphor for hope, about
which Johnson was always sceptical (see the famous opening of
his novel, *Rasselas*).

   But Johnson does not linger on this opening note of self-pity.
He goes on to record the fact of Levet's death. He was, we are
told, 'officious'—that is, helpful, obliging, willing to take trouble
for others. Even though dead he still brings tears to the eyes of
those who loved him. He was 'obscurely wise'—that is, his know-
ledge was not recognized in medical circles. His methods were
coarse (he had no ingratiating bedside manner) and 'unrefin'd'.
He was in fact not professionally qualified since we gather that
he had no letters after his name. Indeed this is clear from the title
and subtitle to the poem. The appeal to 'letter'd arrogance' con-
tains a passing sneer at the medical establishment. In stanza 4
Johnson once more insists, in a neat epigram, on Levet's plain
manners and simplicity of method—'the power of art [that is,

medical skill] without the show'. Levet went out of his way, Johnson continues, to minister to the obscurely miserable and the lonely. He earned a modest livelihood without being slow to answer a call or turning down a case through pride because the fee was trifling. He was a man of virtue—no doubt a practising Christian, whose use of his moderate skill would have been approved by God. In the last two stanzas Johnson reverts from the enumeration of Levet's good qualities to the manner of his death.

The questions to be asked after understanding the poem are: first, how deeply felt is it? Secondly, to what extent does it transcend and triumph over the limitations of the form and manner adopted by Johnson? To take the second question first, readers who do not greatly care for the personifications of eighteenth-century poetry will be put off by the constant use of expressions such as 'fainting nature', 'hov'ring death', 'hopeless anguish' and 'lonely want'. Typical also of eighteenth-century poetic diction are phrases such as 'affection's eye' and 'letter'd arrogance'. So is the periphrasis 'th' Eternal Master'. So too is the comparative absence of graphic detail and concrete imagery, as in line 3. What are 'sudden blasts' and 'slow decline'? This is not how a modern poet would express Johnson's meaning. It was part of eighteenth-century practice to generalize, not to particularize. 'Well tried through many a varying year' does not give us a picture of any precision. In what details, we may wonder, was Levet's kindness coarse and his merit 'unrefin'd'? What were Levet's 'modest wants'? We read through the poem in vain for graphic detail. (As a contrast, look at an earlier eighteenth-century poem, p. 26.) This was the principal feature of late Augustan poetry against which the Romantics reacted. But if we judge the poem by Johnson's own standards, not ours, we see that it has considerable merit. He was opposed to the standards of such pre-Romantic poets as Gray, regarding their poetry as undisciplined, inclined to mawkish displays of passionate feeling. Poetry was to Johnson something formal, even cool. Above all he believed it must conform to canons of propriety. A gentleman did not give way to hysterical grief in public; nor must a poem, since a poem was a public statement, not a private confession. To this can be traced one of the poem's chief merits: it is unexhibitionistic and dwells, not on a self-indulgent display of Johnson's own grief, but on the excellencies of his dead friend. The decorum which Johnson's view of poetry exacts, though it imposes a severe limitation, nevertheless goes with manliness and dignity. The memory of a good, though obscure, man is thus preserved in an attractive form for posterity. The good doctor survives in a brief and worthy memorial.

Notable, too, is the extent to which Johnson achieves warmth without sentimentality (he admits Levet's shortcomings) and graceful expression without affectation. Plenty of graceful verse compliments were composed in Johnson's century, and many of them are cold, insincere, affected and too prone to display the composer's skill. Johnson avoids all these pitfalls, yet never strays beyond the limits of decorum. Johnson was a better critic than a poet, and this is a critic's poem. It is also a moralist's poem. He is not only mourning a dead friend, he is celebrating both moral virtue as he conceives it and poetic propriety according to his critical beliefs. There is a hint of indignation against the artificiality and cupidity of some better-qualified members of the medical profession. It is not a great poem but it is certainly a good one, and the question of its sincerity scarcely needs to be raised. The poetic expression of passionate grief was not in Johnson's repertoire, nor would he have wished it to be. But this is far from saying that there is a lack of feeling. It is impossible to read the poem aloud (as it should be read) without exposing the depth of Johnson's feelings—feelings not diminished by the reserve with which they are expressed. It was because Johnson the man was too emotional, not because he was deficient in emotion, that he avoided giving way to it in his published writings. The control of feeling is very much in the minds of poets of today, as it was in the later Augustan age. It was because they felt that control had led to neutralization and to the atrophy of natural feelings that poets of the Romantic movement rebelled against Augustan canons. There is today a danger that the revolt against feeling among some younger poets will result in the death of feeling. Already in some quarters the need for a new Romantic revival is being felt.

9. EMILY BRONTË: *I am the only being whose doom . . .*

I am the only being whose doom
No tongue would ask, no eye would mourn;
I never caused a thought of gloom,
A smile of joy, since I was born.

In secret pleasure, secret tears,   5
This changeful life has slipped away,
As friendless after eighteen years,
As lone as on my natal day.

There have been times I cannot hide,
There have been times when this was drear,   10
When my sad soul forgot its pride
And longed for one to love me here.

But those were in the early glow
Of feelings since subdued by care;
And they have died so long ago,   15
I hardly now believe they were.

First melted off the hope of youth,
Then fancy's rainbow fast withdrew;
And then experience told me truth
In mortal bosoms never grew.   20

'Twas grief enough to think mankind
All hollow, servile, insincere;
But worse to trust to my own mind
And find the same corruption there.

Emily Brontë wrote many of her poems in the persons of various
of the characters she and her sisters invented in a kind of grand
game that was really much more than a game. But it does not
much profit us to consider the poems in the context of this game,
for the best of them, such as this, stand on their own.

However, in order to gain the full effect from this poem it is

necessary to analyse and discuss its grammatical meaning care-
fully.

The speaker defines himself (or herself), in the first stanza, as
being a curiously neutral and unique creature: he is the *only* one
whose doom nobody would either want or regret; he has never
caused anybody either grief or pleasure since his birth.

This opening stanza is dramatically effective because straight
away our interest is aroused. What kind of person can this be?

The succeeding stanzas tell us more. His life, though so far
brief, has been full of change; and his own pleasures and griefs
have been 'secret'. He has had no friends. It is specifically stated
that he is eighteen years old, although, as we shall see, he is a
very 'old' eighteen.

In the third stanza we are for the first time given some clue as
to the nature of the speaker: his soul is 'sad', and it is implied that
his unhappiness is caused by pride. There have been occasions,
reluctantly owned to, when the friendless state that resulted
from pride was painful ('drear') and when he longed to be loved.

However, these times when pride failed and love was yearned
for occurred in 'the early glow' of emotions that have now been
deadened by anxiety and trouble; he can hardly remember them.
This 'care' that has subdued the early feelings is perhaps melo-
dramatic rather than dramatic: but the speaker is apparently only
eighteen years old, and such melodrama is very much the property
of late adolescence. Few of us have felt older or more oppressed
by care than when we were eighteen. Still, this eighteen-year-old's
situation is particularly bleak: the hope of youth has vanished,
no escape may be had into fancy, and he is even convinced by
'experience' that human beings are incapable of apprehending
the truth. One asks at this point what 'experience' has taught this
friendless, lonely and proud young person that humanity and
truth do not mix? And the question is answered in the final stanza:
his misanthropy, based upon passive observation, had been hard
enough to bear; but worse had been to find the same corruption
in himself.

What is the nature of this corruption? Certainly it is 'hollow,
servile, insincere', but it may also consist of the pride that kept
the speaker apart from others.

Can we quite believe in the black pessimism of this poem?—
or could we if we did not know it came from the author of
Wuthering Heights? There is no doubt that its bleakness is not
always expressed in an inspired manner: 'the hope of youth' and
'fancy's rainbow' are clichés; so even is the phrase applied to
mankind, 'hollow, servile, insincere'. These are weaknesses, since
in poetry we look for precise definitions, not clichés.

But the lonely situation described by the speaker is extremely
unusual, and also completely convincing, and this gives it a
power and strength that it would otherwise lack. Basically, the
poem describes—not always profoundly but none the less truth-
fully—a state of alienation from humanity (see p. 7). (We do
know, of course, that Emily Brontë had such feelings, and that
she expressed them in her great antinomian novel, *Wuthering
Heights*; but here we are judging the poem on its own.)

This sense of alienation is so powerfully conveyed that even
the clichés are given some life. They are not justified, but rather
reflect the fact that the speaker has not subjected his misanthropic
feelings to any very protracted analysis. However, the author
herself does *feel* through the clichés. The analysis of her feelings
came in *Wuthering Heights*, which is a greater achievement than
this poem.

This is a poem that is not altogether successful, but is never-
theless effective because of the writer's sincerity. Some modern
critics have dismissed the notion of sincerity in literature as
meaningless and irrelevant. But clearly it is an important factor
in recognizing the exact merits of this poem.

10. HENRY HOWARD, EARL OF SURREY: *A Tribute to Thomas Clere*

> Norfolk sprang thee, Lambeth holds thee dead,
> Clere, of the County of Cleremont, though hight.
> Within the womb of Ormonds race thou bred,
> And sawest thy cousin crowned in thy sight.
> Shelton for love, Surrey for lord, thou chase;—   5
> Aye, me! while life did last that league was tender.
> Tracing whose steps thou sawest Kelsall blaze,
> Laundersey burnt, and battered Bullen render.
> At Muttrel gates, hopeless of all recure,
> Thine Earl, half dead, gave in thy hand his will;   10
> Which cause did thee this pining death procure,
> Ere summers four times seven thou couldst fulfill.
> Ah, Clere! if love had booted, care, or cost,
> Heaven had not wonne, nor earth so timely lost.

Henry Howard, Earl of Surrey (1517–47), was executed by Henry VIII for high treason, after he had behaved recklessly, but not treasonably. He was a distinguished courtier, soldier and poet; his translation of Books II and III of the *Aeneid* is the first blank verse to be written in English. He was also the author of some beautiful elegiac poems, including three on the death of Sir Thomas Wyatt (see p. 40), who was almost certainly a close friend (in spite of political differences), and the sonnet printed here.

These lines are an elegy for Surrey's squire, Thomas Clere, who gave his life for his master at the siege of Montreuil in 1544.

'Sprang' here means 'brought forth'. Clere is buried in the Howards' chapel at Lambeth; though called ('hight') Clere of the County of Cleremont, he was related to the Howard family. He loved Mary Shelton, a lady-in-waiting at Henry VIII's court; 'chase' means 'chosest'. Kelsall, Laundersey and Bullen (Boulogne) refer to campaigns in which master and squire served together. By 'Muttrel' Surrey means 'Montreuil', where he himself was wounded; Clere died helping him. 'Recure' means 'recovery', or 'remedy'. 'Booted' means 'profited', in the sense of 'mattered'.

It has been suggested that this poem is ineffective, being no more than a tedious rehearsal of complex and no longer relevant genealogical and other information. Yet this is not a valid objection, for the poem affects the majority of its readers. It is interesting to enquire into the reasons for this.

First, Surrey was a most accomplished writer of verse; there is a distinctive music in this sonnet. Note the skilful variations of vowel sounds, by which no two similar sounds are allowed to run together. The great and famous names of men and places, at all times evocative in English poetry, roll off the tongue as if they really meant something: the poet convinces us that he has known these men, been to those places. One thinks of the comparatively small Tudor world, and of the adventurous far-offness of the places.

The subject-matter of the sonnet is very simple: Surrey's regret for the death of the man whom he had loved and who was so devoted to him that he died for him. This is, of course, serious subject-matter. It is difficult to express simple and serious emotion in effective poetry. But Surrey avoids the commonplace and the sentimental by maintaining a beauty of diction and an utter straightforwardness of sense, which exactly matches the tragic simplicity of the theme. The line 'Ere summers four times seven thou couldst fulfill' avoids banality because of its directness and its pathos (even if the 's' sounds are not as well handled as they might be). It is justified, too, by its position in the poem: it convinces us, as an outcry, of the waste that has been involved in this noble death.

It was for love of his master that Clere died; and Surrey says that if 'love', which he personifies in line 13, 'care, or cost', had 'booted' (been any use), then Clere would not have died. But note that a certain paradoxical tone is introduced in the concluding couplet. The penultimate word of the poem is not, as we might expect, 'untimely', but its exact opposite, 'timely'. The meaning of the couplet is that, since 'love' does not, on earth, 'boot', therefore it is better for Clere to be dead, and in heaven. But, because the poem is a tribute to a beloved servant, rather than a personal statement of mood, the bitterness is, so to speak, smuggled in. This is an example of aristocratic good manners in poetry.

Here we have a powerfully evocative poem that gains its effect from being written out of personal circumstances—out of a personal grief. Its theme being simple, the purity of the feeling that occasioned it is apparent in its pellucid and mellifluous surface —in the meaningful use of great names, and the clarity of the diction.

II. SIR THOMAS WYATT: *There was never nothing more me payned . . .*

There was never nothing more me payned,
    Nor nothing more me moved,
As when my swete hert her complayned
    That ever she me loved.
        Alas the while!   5

With pituous loke she saide and sighed:
    Alas, what aileth me
To love and set my welth so light
    On hym that loveth not me?
        Alas the while!   10

Was I not well voyde of all pain,
    When that nothing me greved?
And nowe with sorrous I must complain,
    And cannot be releved.
        Alas the while!   15

My restful nyghtes and joyfull daies
    Syns I began to love
Be take from me; all thing decayes,
    Yet can I not remove.
        Alas the while!   20

She wept and wrong her handes withall,
    The teres fell in my nekke;
She torned her face and let it fall;
    Scarsely therewith coulde speke.
        Alas the while!   25

Her paynes tormented me so sore
    That comfort had I none,
But cursed my fortune more and more
    To se her sobbe and grone:
        Alas the while!   30

'What's wrong with me that I've thought so little of myself and fallen for a man who doesn't love me? I was all right before I met you—not a care in the world. Am I sorry for myself? There's nothing to be done about it. I can't get to sleep thinking of you. I get no fun out of it, but I can't help myself. How blue can you be?'

This, in commonplace modern terms, is roughly what the young lady is saying as she weeps in her lover's arms. The lover, though sorry for her and sorry for himself for being in such a situation, can do nothing to help her. He is out of love with her. The relationship will soon end, but he has enough compassion and humanity to be sorry for both of them.

This is an early Tudor poem about a personal situation between a man and a woman which is common in all ages. This is why we are so often struck by the 'modernity' of Wyatt, a nobleman and diplomat in the service of Henry VIII, who lived and died over four hundred years ago. It is, if you like, a simple poem, but it has a directness and a sureness of psychological touch which are rare enough in poetry at any time and very rare, if not unique, in Wyatt's time. Is the young man sorrier for himself or for the woman? This is a question to which the answer is not to be found in the poem. We cannot doubt his sincerity when he says that this touching incident grieved him and moved him more than anything had ever done. Yet perhaps a different interpretation is possible. Perhaps it is not 'the end of the affair'. Perhaps it is no more than a lovers' quarrel. If this is so, we must admit that the lady is playing her cards skilfully. How many young men have been persuaded to a return of loverly attention by a young lady's somewhat over-dramatic outbursts of self-reproach at having allowed herself to fall in love with, to lose sleep over, a man who doesn't care for her (and, of course, *vice versa*).

We are given the incident, recounted no doubt faithfully, and allowed to draw our own conclusions. This is a light and subtle poem, not over-elaborated, not worked out in depth, and each reader is entitled to his own interpretation.

To return to our original approximate modern paraphrase of the lady's words: neither this nor any other good poem consists only of its meaning, the sense of what it says. You may translate her words into any idiom you like—that of a 'pop' song, for instance, or a Restoration lyric. But the effect and point of the poem are the poem itself: the lady's words, the lover's comments, the grave and measured rhythm of the verse, the sad repetition of the sigh 'Alas the while' (a common Tudor phrase). It is all this, not simply the psychology, the sex play, that makes the poem. Wyatt's lyrics were written for the lute, and this probably helped the rhythm. He wrote at a time when the English language was in process of transition, and accents and pronunciation were in a fluid state. For a long time after the sixteenth century it was supposed that he had a bad ear and that his rhythms were uncertain. This was not the case; but we read poetry aloud differently today. In reading this we should adopt a somewhat free rhythm and not expect the lines to march as to a simple pattern.

We have taken note of the 'modernity' of the poem, and it is right to stress this while noting also the points of difference between Tudor verse and modern English. To our ears the double negative in line 1 may seem strange: this feature was common up to and after Shakespeare's time, half a century later. In line 8 '*welth*' means 'well being', 'peace of mind'. In line 19 'remove' is now archaic, meaning 'change'. Allowing for these and a few other terms and expressions strange to our ears, this is a poem which, more than most, can help us to forget the centuries between us and our Tudor ancestors.

O doe not die, for I shall hate
    All women so, when thou art gone,
That thee I shall not celebrate,
    When I remember, thou wast one.

But yet thou canst not die, I know;   5
    To leave this world behinde, is death,
But when thou from this world wilt goe,
    The whole world vapors with thy breath.

Or if, when thou, the worlds soule, goest,
    It stay, 'tis but thy carkasse then,   10
The fairest woman, but thy ghost,
    But corrupt wormes, the worthyest men.

O wrangling schooles, that search what fire
    Shall burne this world, had none the wit
Unto this knowledge to aspire,   15
    That this her feaver might be it?

And yet she cannot wast by this,
    Nor long beare this torturing wrong,
For much corruption needfull is
    To fuell such a feaver long.   20

These burning fits but meteors bee,
    Whose matter in thee is soone spent.
Thy beauty, 'and* all parts, which are thee,
    Are unchangeable firmament.

Yet 'twas of my minde, seising thee,   25
    Though it in thee cannot persever.
For I had rather owner bee
    Of thee one houre, then all else ever.

This is a characteristically 'metaphysical' poem by the most
famous, indeed, the paradigm of, the 'metaphysical poets'. The

* The inverted comma indicates an elision.

seventeenth-century laird, inventor and poet William Drummond first applied the term to poetry; Dryden first used it of the poetry of Donne; and Dr Johnson, in his *Life of Cowley*, made it famous: 'The metaphysical poets were men of learning,' he wrote, 'and to show their learning was their whole aim.' The term is useful in that it isolates a certain element in their poetry: a use of elaborate argument, an emphasis upon thought as distinct from feeling (though feeling is not absent), a drawing of a scientific type of knowledge into the service of poetry.

This poem may well strike us as being excessively metaphysical, although the hyperbole of the world being destroyed by the death of a mistress has its origin in a poem by the fourteenth-century Italian poet, Petrarch. Its immediate occasion is that the poet's mistress is suffering from a fever: if she dies, Donne says, then he will never love any woman again. The argument is: If you die, then every woman I see will remind me of my grief, and so I shall hate your whole sex.

In the next stanzas Donne says that his mistress cannot die, however: for her, there is no death: she will leave her memory behind her; the most beautiful woman will be no more than her ghost, and the most gifted men will be but corrupt worms.

Did not these wrangling theologians, he goes on to say, who argue about what fire will finally destroy this world (that the world would be destroyed by fire, and in the seventeenth century, was believed by certain theologians of the time)—did they not realize that his mistress' fever was the answer to their question?

Yet this fever cannot waste her for long: great corruption would be needed to feed such a fever for long, and her beauty is heavenly and therefore incorruptible: her spasms of fever are as brief as shooting stars. And yet this temporary illness did to her exactly what the poet would have done: it seized her for the short period of which alone it was capable—just as the poet would rather be the possessor of her for an hour than anything else for ever.

The reader is bound to ask, is this merely extravagant, or does it add something to our understanding of the experience of love? We may well concede that it does. For there is always, to a lover, something in the beloved that seems impossible to possess; and it is this aspect of romantic love that makes it like a fever. The feverish aspect of love is, in a sense, a disease that might tend to destroy the beloved; yet a true lover will recognize this and will acknowledge the superiority of the beloved. Thus the fever is described by Donne as a 'torturing wrong' ('torturing' is accented on the second syllable), and is even compared with the true nature of the hell which theologians seek to define. The poem has strong feeling as well as being characterized by involved thought; the ending is lyrical and certainly rounds off the thinking with a firm and convincing emotion. It has been said that very few poets do not leave their intellects behind when they fall in love; Donne is perhaps the supreme intellectual of English love poetry—a statement that this poem does much to justify. We cannot doubt the sincerity of his passion; yet some would say that *A Feaver* is too contrived and rhetorical to be wholly genuine. What do you think?

13. EDMUND BLUNDEN: *Report on Experience*

I have been young, and now am not too old;
And I have seen the righteous forsaken,
His health, his honour and his quality taken.
    This is not what we were formerly told.

I have seen a green country, useful to the race,   5
Knocked silly with guns and mines, its villages vanished,
Even the last rat and last kestrel vanished—
    God bless us all, this was peculiar grace.

I knew Seraphina; Nature gave her hue,
Glance, sympathy, note, like one from Eden.   10
I saw her smile warp, heard her lyric deaden;
    She turned to harlotry;—this I took to be new.

Say what you will, our God sees how they run.
These disillusions are His curious proving
That He loves humanity and will go on loving;   15
    Over there are faith, life, virtue in the sun.

This powerful poem, written out of the experiences of its author in World War One, achieves its effect by skilful and sensitive manipulations of tone. But it is important to realize that such an effect could not have been achieved without the initial impetus of a very strong emotion: a despair that, in life, beauty and goodness are frequently defeated by evil. We might, even if unfashionably, describe the impetus of this initial emotion as inspiration.

The bitter, ironic sharpness of stanza 1 sets the tone of the whole poem. The first clause, 'I have been young', ironically exploits a cliché—it should be remembered that much of the blame for the miseries of World War One was attributed to the old and allegedly 'experienced', to just the kind of people who are in the habit of saying 'I have been young'. For it is followed by the restrained but crushingly bitter 'and now am not too old'.

The implication is, of course, that the poet has had experiences that have aged him beyond his years. The next three lines need no explaining: they are straightforward. They contrast the comfortable and comforting teachings of an older generation with the results of its actions.

Stanza 2, again, is straightforward, reserving its irony for the last line. The phrase 'useful to the race' is the sort used in the 'education' against which this poem complains. The third stanza is more personal: it parallels the universal experience with private and sexual experience. The name 'Seraphina' is chosen to illustrate the apparent perfection of the woman the poet has loved: a seraph is a member of the highest order of the angels. The last statement, 'this I took to be new', achieves its effect from a directness in which there is a note of ironic understatement. It inevitably reminds the reader of his own first disillusions in love and in life, and of how he, too, naively took them to be 'new'.

The final stanza states the poet's conclusion. The 'Say what you will', apparently rhetorical, reminds us that the theme of this poem is the difference between words and actions, false teachings and true experience. The teachers—this includes all our 'elders and betters'—often appeal to conventional notions of God; the poet shows us a different, even a Hardyesque (see p. 62) kind of God. Here is a God who, like the farmer's wife in the nursery-rhyme, slaughters humanity—which is compared, by implication, to 'blind mice'.

The final three lines of the poem, although imbued with sadness and bitterness, are not simply ironic. They attack the conventional notion of God, but at the same time they acknowledge the existence of beauty and goodness, and love that does not betray. Otherwise how could we become disillusioned? Thus, the last line states that faith, life (as opposed to the carnage of war) and virtue exist 'Over there'.

Where is 'Over there'? The point of the phrase is its vagueness. But if the poet had wished to be wholly ironic, wholly despairing, he might well have written 'up there', i.e. in heaven. For certainly the idea of heaven cannot be said to exist 'Over there'. No, somewhere on earth, within ourselves perhaps, life and faith and virtue do exist. At the same time, 'Over there' may refer to

France, where so many of Blunden's contemporaries are lying dead. Yet some small hope gleams through the flat, dignified bitterness. For so many of those not disillusioned, dead young men really were faithful, vital and virtuous. The false cliché that they sacrificed their lives for their country, the kind of cliché found in such specious verse as Rupert Brooke's '*If I should die*' sonnet (admittedly written before the real nature of the war had become apparent to any but a very few), is avoided; but the correct notion that they died in vain is emphasized. However, their innocent state of illusion did exist, and in that, paradoxically, there is some hope.

For two other poems arising from experiences in World War One see p. 134.

BEN JONSON: *To the Memory of my Beloved, the Author,*
Mr. William Shakespeare: and what he hath left us

To draw no envy (Shakespeare) on thy name,
Am I thus ample to thy Booke, and Fame:
While I confesse thy writings to be such,
As neither Man, nor Muse, can praise too much.
'Tis true, and all mens suffrage. But these wayes   5
Were not the paths I meant unto thy praise:
For seeliest Ignorance on these may light,
Which, when it sounds at best, but eccho's right;
Or blinde Affection, which doth ne're advance
The truth, but gropes, and urgeth all by chance;   10
Or crafty Malice, might pretend this praise,
And thinke to ruine, where it seem'd to raise.
These are, as some infamous Baud, or Whore,
Should praise a Matron. What could hurt her more?
But thou art proofe against them, and indeed   15
Above th' ill fortune of them, or the need.
I therefore will begin. Soule of the Age!
The applause! delight! the wonder of our Stage!
My Shakespeare, rise; I will not lodge thee by
Chaucer, or Spenser, or bid Beaumont lye   20
A little further, to make thee a roome:
Thou art a Moniment, without a tombe,
And art alive still, while thy Booke doth live,
And we have wits to read, and praise to give.
That I not mixe thee so, my braine excuses;   25
I meane with great, but disproportion'd Muses:
For, if I thought my judgement were of yeeres,
I should commit thee surely with thy peeres,
And tell, how farre thou didst our Lily out-shine,
Or sporting Kid, or Marlowes mighty line.   30
And though thou hadst small Latine, and lesse Greeke,
From thence to honour thee, I would not seeke
For names; but call forth thund'ring Æschilus,
Euripides, and Sophocles to us,
Paccuvius, Accius, him of Cordova dead,   35
To life againe, to heare thy Buskin tread,

And shake a Stage: Or, when thy Sockes were on,
Leave thee alone, for the comparison
Of all, that insolent Greece, or haughtie Rome
Sent forth, or since did from their ashes come.   40
Triumph, my Britaine, thou hast one to showe,
To whom all Scenes of Europe homage owe.
He was not of an age, but for all time!
And all the Muses still were in their prime,
When like Apollo he came forth to warme   45
Our eares, or like a Mercury to charme!
Nature her selfe was proud of his designes,
And joy'd to weare the dressing of his lines!
Which were so richly spun, and woven so fit,
As, since, she will vouchsafe no other Wit.   50
The merry Greeke, tart Aristophanes,
Neat Terence, witty Plautus, now not please;
But antiquated, and deserted lye
As they were not of Natures family.
Yet must I not give Nature all: Thy Art,   55
My gentle Shakespeare, must enjoy a part.
For though the Poets matter, Nature be,
His Art doth give the fashion. And, that he,
Who casts to write a living line, must sweat,
(Such as thine are) and strike the second heat   60
Upon the Muses anvile: turne the same,
(And himselfe with it) that he thinkes to frame;
Or for the lawrell, he may gaine a scorne,
For a good Poet's made, as well as borne.
And such wert thou. Looke how the fathers face   65
Lives in his issue, even so, the race
Of Shakespeares minde, and manners brightly shines
In his well torned, and true-filed lines:
In each of which, he seemes to shake a Lance,
As brandish't at the eyes of Ignorance.   70
Sweet Swan of Avon! what a sight it were
To see thee in our waters yet appeare,
And make those flights upon the bankes of Thames,
That so did take Eliza, and our James!
But stay, I see thee in the Hemisphere   75
Advanc'd, and made a Constellation there!
Shine forth, thou Starre of Poets, and with rage,

Or influence, chide, or cheere the drooping Stage;
Which, since thy flight from hence, hath mourn'd like night,
And despaires day, but for thy Volumes light.   80

It is a fairly common experience to find that although you know
many of the individual phrases in this poem, some of which have
become clichés, you do not know the poem as a whole—or,
perhaps, that the famous phrases first occurred in it. The poem
was first printed in the First Folio, which contained all Shake-
speare's plays (except *Pericles*), in 1623. Jonson, who was a per-
sonal friend of Shakespeare's, was the most illustrious living
writer. This is not a difficult poem, except that the senses in
which Jonson employed some of the words and phrases are no
longer familiar. We need to understand it fully before we can
appreciate its rare distinction. It is the kind of expository, some-
what rambling, conversational poem that Jonson was particularly
good at writing.

To 'draw' means here to 'bring'; 'all mens suffrage' means that
everyone agrees with Jonson's verdict (this poem is one of the
very few pieces of evidence we possess as to Shakespeare's stand-
ing in his own lifetime; it is also, in itself, a complete refutation
of all theories that anyone other than Shakespeare himself wrote
the plays). 'Seeliest' is probably fused by Jonson in its senses of
'most miserable', and 'silly'. In these lines Jonson seems to have
foreseen that Shakespeare's work would become the object of
much undiscriminating and insincere worship. Jonson's argument
is that praise of Shakespeare should be truthful, and not ignorant,
blindly affectionate (Jonson told William Drummond in 1618
that he worshipped Shakespeare 'but this side idolatry') or cun-
ningly malicious. Beaumont is the dramatist Francis Beaumont,
who wrote many popular and very successful plays in collabora-
tion with John Fletcher. Paccuvius and Accius were Latin
tragedians of the second century B.C.; 'him of Cordova dead'
refers to Seneca, another important Latin playwright. The 'Bus-
kin' was a half-boot worn in tragedy, often contrasted with the
'sock' worn in comedy. 'Buskin' and 'sock' came to mean, figura-
tively, the tragic and the comic vein respectively.

In line 60 the phrase 'second heat' arises from Jonson's belief

that while the first heat, or poetic authenticity, of poetry comes
from natural inspiration, it needs some art to retain its effective-
ness. 'For a good Poet's made, as well as borne' deliberately
recalls a line from one of the poems of Horace, whose work
Jonson knew well, 'poeta nascitur non fit'. 'Shake a Lance' puns,
of course, on the name 'Shakespeare'. Jonson seems to suggest
that Shakespeare's work is reminiscent of the man. 'Flights' puns
on the senses 'flights of a bird' and 'flights of poetry', and the
next line refers to the fact that both Queen Elizabeth and King
James enjoyed (were 'taken'—captivated—by) some of Shakes-
peare's plays. 'Rage' here means *furor poeticus*, poetic inspiration,
as well as anger (at the inferior plays of the time).

In the land of turkeys in turkey weather
At the base of the statue, we go round and round.
What a beautiful history, beautiful surprise!
Monsieur is on horseback. The horse is covered with mice.

This dance has no name. It is a hungry dance.   5
We dance it out to the tip of Monsieur's sword,
Reading the lordly language of the inscription,
Which is like zithers and tambourines combined:

The Founder of the State. Whoever founded
A state that was free, in the dead of winter, from mice?   10
What a beautiful tableau tinted and towering,
The arm of bronze outstretched against all evil!

This is a gay, lively, witty trifle which at first sight makes little sense. It concerns a crowd of mice dancing around and all over a bronze equestrian statue. The bronze rider has a sword, and on the base of the statue is a lordly and jubilant inscription.

But this is not all. Under the apparently frivolous surface there are more serious implications. There are also apparent obscurities, amounting at first sight even to wilful extravagance. We read of 'a beautiful history'. What has history to do with this dance? The dance is described as 'hungry'. The hunger is connected with the cold of winter. The inscription on the statue's base is 'lordly' and jubilant. Who is this 'Founder of the State' whose arm, grasping its sword, is 'outstretched against all evil!'? Moreover, there is an initial difficulty. What is 'the land of turkeys', 'turkey weather'?

It is this first line that offers the key to the whole poem, for the only country that can be described as 'land of turkeys' is the United States. (It can scarcely be Turkey itself, which has little connection with turkeys, except that the bird was once erroneously supposed to originate there.) The eating of turkeys by Americans on Thanksgiving Day (the last Thursday in

November—'turkey weather') is a custom that goes back to pre-revolutionary days. It marks the gratitude of the original settlers on the eastern seaboard of America for their deliverance after the voyage from England and the finding of the native American turkey, a prime supplier of food.

Why is the original of the bronze statue referred to as 'Monsieur'? Clearly this is a Frenchman associated with the foundation of the United States. This can be no other than the Frenchman, the Marquis de Lafayette, a revolutionary French patriot who did much to help the Americans in their struggle against British colonial rule. America took him to its heart and made him a hero of the state, almost its 'Founder'. The inscription on the statue no doubt announces in its 'lordly language' the triumph of freedom and democracy. Here we begin to note the ironical tone of the poem, the implied contrast between the statue and what it stands for, on the one hand, and the hungry dance of mice, the most diminutive of creatures, in the cold weather of a hungry November. We do not think of America as a hungry and starving country, but there have been times of great poverty and hardship, notably the 'depression' of the early 1930's

It is reasonable, then, to infer that the humorously ironical mind of the poet sees American latterday democracy as a somewhat ghoulish dance of numerous but insignificant beings about a statue symbolizing American idealism as represented by the eighteenth-century 'Founder of the State'. 'This is what American democratic ideals have come to,' the poem seems to say, '—a hungry dance of insignificant beings about a statue representing national aspirations in all their jubilant purity.'

We see then how Stevens characteristically compresses a considerable area of suggestion into a small compass, and how he can treat with elegant lightness a grave and important subject. It would be a mistake to take the political or social implications of the poem too seriously. Here, as frequently, Stevens carries his seriousness lightly. There is nothing portentous about the free verse-form adopted by Stevens, nor about the precise, careful, yet unexaggerated language of the poem.

She wore a wreath of roses,
    The night that first we met,
Her lovely face was smiling,
    Beneath her curls of jet.
Her footstep had the lightness,   5
    Her voice the joyous tone;
The tokens of a youthful heart,
    Where sorrow is unknown.
I saw her but a moment,
    Yet methinks I see her now,   10
With the wreath of summer flowers,
    Upon her snowy brow.

A wreath of orange blossoms,
    When next we met, she wore;
The expression of her features   15
    Was more thoughtful than before.
And standing by her side was one,
    Who strove, and not in vain,
To soothe her, leaving that dear home
    She ne'er might view again.   20
I saw her but a moment,
    Yet methinks I see her now,
With the wreath of orange blossoms,
    Upon her snowy brow.

And once again I see that brow,   25
    No bridal wreath is there,
The widow's sombre cap conceals
    Her once luxuriant hair.
She weeps in silent solitude,
    And there is one near   30
To press her hand within his own,
    And wipe away the tear.
I see her broken hearted,
    Yet methinks I see her now,
In the pride of youth and beauty,   35
    With a garland on her brow.

There are several kinds and degrees of badness in poetry. It would be depressing, even morbid, to spend a lot of time weighing and measuring them, but it is as well sometimes to examine our own reactions to an obviously bad poem and test our ability to say just why it is bad. If not, we are always in danger of being taken in by the spurious and wasting time on inferior art.

Thomas Haynes Bayly (1797–1839), who is not represented by a single poem in *The Oxford Book of English Romantic Verse*, a comprehensive anthology of the period, was once very popular, one might say universally read, sung and recited throughout the Victorian age.

She wore a wreath of roses is a bad poem, but it was enjoyed by readers who were not more liable to be taken in than many readers of today. To us its badness is obvious because it is not the sort of badness that goes down today. The sentiment is warm and over-ripe, and modern readers prefer cleverness and coolness, a sour, rather than a ripe tone. The Victorians (note, by the way, that Bayly was not a Victorian; he was one of those who set the fashion for that age) liked an atmosphere of roses and orange-blossom, which we are entitled to call sentimental. There is nothing intrinsically poetic about such an atmosphere. Some modern readers take the opposite view, that kitchen sinks and festering sores are intrinsically poetic. This is simply inverted sentimentality. The truth is that poetry is not substantially an affair of subject-matter. It is an affair of feelings about subject-matter, and Bayly's poem has at least the outward appearance of being concerned with feeling. What, then, is wrong with it? Why is it bad?

First, it must be said that technically, or at least in construction, it is competent verse. Bayly had an easy flow of smooth, often natural verse, in the manner of his contemporary Tom Moore of the still popular *Irish Melodies*. He is not easily faulted on rhythm and word order, though line 14 ('When next we met, she wore') is not wholly satisfactory. (If the order had been more natural, Bayly would have had trouble with his rhyme.) It is in his diction that Bayly gives himself away as a hack. No real poet could allow himself a succession of clichés such as 'curls of jet' 'not in vain', 'snowy' and 'methinks'. These were clichés even in Bayly's time. Where the diction is not cliché-ridden, it is generally commonplace.

When we look beneath the surface, we discover a more radical fault—that of obscurity. This is not the obscurity of a poet such as Donne or Hopkins, whose apparent difficulty yields to close attention and is the result of complex thought and emotion. It is an obscurity which strives to cover up a genuine lack of meaning. In stanza 1 we learn of the poet's first glimpse of a joyful, care-free, black-haired girl, whom he met at night for 'but a moment'. The occasion seems to have been a significant one, but we learn no more of this. Was it love at first sight? We are not told.

The poet next turns up at the girl's wedding. Again he insists that they 'met', though only long enough for him to glimpse a new thoughtfulness in her and see the bridegroom comforting her over leaving the home 'She ne'er might view again'. What were his feelings? Jealousy, grief, envy? Your guess is as good as ours. Why couldn't the happy couple visit the parents' home after marriage?

In stanza 3 the mystery deepens—the mystery of what part the poet ('I') takes in the story. He now sees the snowy brow surmounted by a widow's cap. We know she is much older, because some of her hair has fallen out. Why is she 'in solitude' and weeping? Her husband is dead, but is she weeping on that account? She has no friends. Even if she had gone abroad after marriage, leaving her home for ever, it seems odd that she had made no friends and had no family of her own to comfort her. If so, why does not the poet ring the door-bell and renew his acquaintance? The question offers itself, does he really *see* her as a widow or is this just fantasy? If so, the final vision of her, clearly a mere flashback, has no meaning at all. Or does it mean simply that he prefers to think of her in her rose-crowned youth? If so, it is the sentimental perversity of one who cannot face the facts and never could.

Whether or not the reader is meant to make sense of the poem by looking for answers to these questions, it is certain that the poet either had no answers to them or that he was dealing with a situation he could not express. Our own view is that there is no situation at all, but that we are meant to think there is. The poem is not based on any actual experience, but is a self-indulgent fantasy, a game with verbal counters. It is a series of riddles to which there are no answers. Yet it deals with important matters —carefree youth, marriage, grief and loneliness; and it seems that we are meant to enjoy the luxury of having emotions for which there is no ground in fact. This is a fair definition of at least one important aspect of sentimentality, which usually involves getting something for nothing. The poet has expended no real emotion in producing the poem, and he is trying to induce spurious emotions in his readers. It is the spurious in poetry, rather than the obviously bad, which is the enemy of the good.

We are all sentimental at times. There is no harm in sentimentality, provided we recognize it and do not regard it as a substitute for feeling. In poetry it usually occurs in a context of fashionably 'poetic' matter—roses, snowy maidens, weeping widows, or, on the other hand, kitchen sinks and surgical operations. There is of course nothing intrinsically poetic—or unpoetic—in any of these things. They can occur in good as well as bad poems. It is the experience of the poet (as well as his skill in making use of it) that determines whether the poem is good or a mere sentimental exploitation of other people's experience. It is one of the hardest tests of a reader's discrimination to be able to detect the spurious in poetry. Why do it? Because we can only make room in our minds for real poetry by clearing away the rubbish. If we cannot face facts in poetry, we may find it harder to face them in life. That is why we have taken up so much space in getting at the inside of a poem which turns out to be more or less worthless. Are we too serious?

My enemy had bidden me as guest.
His table all set out with wine and cake,
His ordered chairs, he to beguile me dressed
So neatly, moved my pity for his sake.

I knew it was an ambush, but could not   5
Leave him to eat his cake up by himself
And put his unused glasses on the shelf.
I made pretence of falling in his plot,

And trembled when in his anxiety
He bared it too absurdly to my view.   10
And even as he stabbed me through and through
I pitied him for his small strategy.

Norman Cameron died in 1953 at the early age of 47. For long treated by the majority of reviewers as one of 'the school of Graves', on the strength of the friendship of the two poets, he has more recently been appreciated as an original poet in his own right. His *Collected Poems*, one of the most distinguished slim volumes of its era, appeared posthumously; it was reprinted in 1967. *The Compassionate Fool* is not one of his richest poems, but it is one of his most characteristic in its deceptive simplicity, its unobtrusive neatness of construction, its irony and its firm basis in personal experience.

This is a poem that tells a story. The words used are unambiguous; the language is not dense or complex. The subtlety of the poem emerges through careful attention to the sardonically expressed paradoxes, of which the first line, 'My enemy had bidden me as guest', is typical. Clearly the narrator of the poem has been invited to be harmed or destroyed—why otherwise should an *enemy* issue an invitation? Next the narrator describes how he felt pity for his enemy: his efforts to deceive—the carefully contrived refreshments, the chairs arranged—were so pathetic. The poet knows that he is going to be ambushed, but feels so sorry for his enemy that he pretends to be taken in, and is even frightened when his enemy makes his plot too obvious. And even while he is being stabbed to death, the fool still feels compassion —not hate—for his murderer's meanness and the clumsiness with which he executes his plan.

This is a most remarkable poem in that it will convincingly and revealingly relate to many aspects of our own experience; it also has a more universal meaning, one which amounts to a valid generalization about experience.

The Compassionate Fool might apply to a love-affair—it might be spoken by a girl who has let her lover seduce her out of pity for him, in which case the word 'stabbed' would assume a well-established phallic significance. It applies to any relationship in which we give up our own life, pleasure, freedom, or desire to another person, not because we are tricked or deceived, but because we lack the ruthlessness to expose the meanness or ineptitude of another's effort to manipulate us or shape us to his will. The compassionate fool is foolish, not because he lacks intelligence but because he sacrifices his own interests for the sake of the sort of pity that arises from understanding. The poem does not suggest that this process is good or bad; it wryly describes it, cynically implying by the metaphor of death by stabbing that it is likely, in a material sense, to be a disastrous process. The cruel moral of this allegorical poem is that it is the stupid and the insensitive, the bad actors, who get on in this world—not because of their own cleverness but because of the compassionate 'foolishness' of their superiors.

But the poem sounds a more optimistic note: the enemy may win when he stabs the fool to death, but the fool who can pity him for his 'small strategy' as he does it, who has pretended to fall for his ploy out of compassion, does enjoy his superiority— otherwise he would suddenly feel sorry for himself as the dagger moved towards him. The conflict is between the insensitive, the man who needs to dominate, the ambitious—and the sensitive: the latter allow themselves to be exploited by their recognition of the humanity of the former (to feel sorry for someone in the manner described here is certainly to recognize his humanity). The poem offers no comment on this situation; it only describes the lot of the intelligent man who allows himself to be guided by his emotions rather than by his self-interest.

18. THOMAS HARDY: *Last Words to a Dumb Friend*

Pet was never mourned as you,
Purrer of the spotless hue,
Plumy tail, and wistful gaze
While you humoured our queer ways,
Or outshrilled your morning call   5
Up the stairs and through the hall—
Foot suspended in its fall—
While, expectant, you would stand
Arched, to meet the stroking hand;
Till your way you chose to wend   10
Yonder, to your tragic end.

Never another pet for me!
Let your place all vacant be;
Better blankness day by day
Than companion torn away.   15
Better bid his memory fade,
Better blot each mark he made,
Selfishly escape distress
By contrived forgetfulness,
Than preserve his prints to make   20
Every morn and eve an ache.

From the chair whereon he sat
Sweep his fur, nor wince thereat;
Rake his little pathways out
Mid the bushes roundabout;   25
Smooth away his talons' mark
From the claw-worn pine-tree bark,
Where he climbed as dusk embrowned,
Waiting us who loitered round.

Strange it is this speechless thing,   30
Subject to our mastering,
Subject for his life and food
To our gift, and time, and mood,
Timid pensioner of us Powers,

His existence ruled by ours,   35
Should—by crossing at a breath
Into safe and shielded death,
By the merely taking hence
Of his insignificance—
Loom as largened to the sense   40
Shape as part, above man's will,
Of the Imperturbable.

As a prisoner, flight debarred,
Exercising in a yard,
Still retain I, troubled, shaken,   45
Mean estate, by him forsaken;
And this home, which scarcely took
Impress from his little look,
By his faring to the Dim
Grows all eloquent of him.   50

Housemate, I can think you still
Bounding to the window-sill,
Over which I vaguely see
Your small mound beneath the tree,
Showing in the autumn shade   55
That you moulder where you played.

The title of this poem is not promising. The British are famous, whether justly or unjustly, for their capacity for sentimentality about pets and concomitant cruel neglect of human miseries. But this poem is not sentimental; it might be said, on the contrary, to effectively isolate the unsentimental from the sentimental elements in our feelings towards household pets, and ultimately to draw a sinister conclusion of a sort most unpalatable to potential members of Our Dumb Friends' League.

The first stanza describes, straightforwardly, the reasons for our affection towards cats and their familiar idiosyncrasies—the foot suspended in its fall, the arched, expectant back. The description has virtue because it is truthful; 'Purrer of the spotless hue' could be said to verge on the sentimental, but is justified by the humorous precision of 'spotless' used unexpectedly in a literal sense, whereas we tend to associate the word with moral

qualities—by this usage Hardy reminds us of his own unsenti-
mentality—and the manner in which the phrase sums up the
kind of feeling those who keep cats have about them—itself some-
times just verging on the sentimental. The only word that may
seem to jar is 'tragic'; 'end', by itself, might seem to be much more
effective, for poets are usually well-advised to omit adjectives
that do no more than attempt to describe the effect the poem as a
whole should make. But we shall see that the end of the poem
justifies the use of the word.

Stanzas 2 and 3 describe the immediate mood evoked by the
loss of a pet; the line most characteristic of this poet is 'Never
another pet for me!' Is this not what we all feel when we have
lost something that we have valued? We determine (usually
vainly) not to put our emotions at risk again.

Stanza 4 demonstrates unequivocally that the poet is fully
aware of the dangers of sentimentality inherent in his theme.
Although his preceding description of grief for this small, non-
human thing has been so poignantly accurate as to remove all
traces of falseness, he nevertheless faces the real issue. Who can
deny that the death of a pet can, if only for a short time, 'Loom
as largened to the sense, / Shape as part, above man's will, / Of
the Imperturbable.'? The Imperturbable is one of this author's
many names for the relentless fate that rules over human affairs.

The thought of the penultimate stanza is somewhat more com-
plicated than that of the preceding. The author speaks of his own
condition, comparing it by implication with that of the cat,
doomed to death like a prisoner 'Exercising in a yard'. He admits
that the essentials of his life have hardly been changed by the
cat ('this home, which scarcely took / Impress from your little
look') but he nevertheless presses his present mood of sorrow
and regret to its logical conclusion: the cat's death has reminded
him of his own and everyone else's mortality, but he insists that,
for the moment, his life is 'all eloquent' of the cat, who in life
did little more than incidentally delight. We are thus reminded
that we ourselves, for all our anthropocentric preoccupations, are
in fact merely a part of nature. Ironically, the cat's real moment
of influence, the time when he really impresses himself, is that of
his death.

The point has been made. But the last stanza returns to the cat itself, because the cat is what originally set off the train of thought. The poet thus rejects abstraction, concretely returning to the original object. Thus, the two sad final lines gain a strength, through poignancy, that they would not otherwise have possessed. The concrete death of a cat seems less serious than that of a human being considered abstractly, but only because we imagine that human beings, because they think they are not 'playing', will do something more after death than merely 'moulder'. This poem suggests otherwise. Hence the previous use of the word 'tragic' to describe the cat's death. By beautifully concentrating our attention upon our actual feelings of grief for a dead pet, the poem cruelly emphasizes the truth of our own condition.

Notice that the poet, despite the apparent egocentricity of his conclusion, keeps his eye on the cat throughout the poem. It is impossible to assert either that he merely exploits the death of the cat in order to draw attention to his own plight as a lonely prisoner, or that he rhetorically inflates its death for a cheap effect. After all, he insists that the cat, for all the delight it gave, owes its existence to its 'master' and was only a cat. Thus, the poem resolves a tension between sympathy with and love for the cat, and the revelation of his own predicament.

Safe in their alabaster chambers,
Untouched by morning
And untouched by noon,
Sleep the meek members of the resurrection—
Rafter of satin, 5
And roof of stone.

Light laughs the breeze
In her castle above them,
Babbles the bee in a stolid ear,
Pipe the sweet birds in ignorant cadence— 10
Ah, what sagacity perished here!

This poem is a commentary on the immensity, the finality of death. It is an expression of the emotions of pity and awe—awe at the absoluteness of death. The dead are referred to as 'Safe in their alabaster chambers'—life is full of risk and uncertainty: death is 'safe'. 'Alabaster' refers to monumental masonry. The dead are immune from the ordinary concerns of day-to-day humanity—'Untouched by morning'. Comment is superfluous on the superb phrase 'the meek members of the resurrection', when it is recalled that Emily Dickinson was a Christian. Death for her was a preparation for the immortality that begins at the resurrection. 'Rafter of satin, / And roof of stone' refers to the lining of a coffin under its stone memorial slab.

Stanza 2, about the breeze in its leafy 'castle', the babbling bees and the indifferent piping birds, expresses with profound pity the fact that the outer world of nature goes on unheeding of the fate that has befallen the dead.

The poem, so far as its first two stanzas go, is thus an expression of resigned and stoical compassion for the dead.

But the poet was not wholly satisfied with her second stanza. She wrote no fewer than three alternative versions of it, and she never decided which was the best. After considering all the alternatives, which do you think is the most satisfactory conclusion?

Alternative versions of second stanza

Grand go the years in the crescent above them,
World scoop their arcs
And firmaments row,
Diadems drop and Doges surrender,
Soundless as dots on a disc of snow.

Springs shake the sills
But the echoes stiffen,
Hoar is the window
And numb the door.
Tribes of eclipse in tents of marble
Staples of ages have buckled there.

Springs shake the seals
But the silence stiffens,
Frosts unhook in the Northern zones,
Icicles crawl from Polar caverns,
Midnight in marble refutes the suns.

[*Notes on alternative versions*
Stanza 1. The first two lines suggest the immensity of external nature. Line 3 suggests the mortality of human systems. 'Doges' evidently refers to rulers in general—the all-powerful ones who must submit in the end to extinction. 'Dots on a disc of snow' means the minute- or second-marks on the white circle of a clock or a watch.

Stanza 2. The thought is that, while in the world outside the grave spring will bring a thaw, no such thaw is possible for the dead.

Stanza 3. Repeats this thought, adding that 'Midnight in marble', i.e. the tomb, 'refutes', i.e. denies, the warming power of spring suns.]

Three thinges there bee that prosper up apace
And flourish, whilest they growe a sunder farr,
But on a day, they meet all in one place,
And when they meet, they one an other marr;
And they bee theise the wood, the weede, the wagg.   5
The wood is that, which makes the Gallow tree,
The weed is that, which stringes the Hangmans bagg,
The wagg my pritty knave betokeneth thee.
Marke well deare boy whilest theise assemble not,
Green springs the tree, hempe growes, the wagg is wilde,   10
But when they meet, it makes the timber rott,
It fretts the halter, and it choakes the childe.

Sir Walter Ralegh (c. 1552–1618) was a man of many parts:
poet, courtier, sailor, soldier, adventurer. . . . He is not an easy
man to understand; but recent research suggests that his character
was somewhat maligned by nineteenth-century historians. As a
poet he anticipated the 'metaphysical' style of Donne by some
years, and he was certainly the most accomplished ironist of his
generation. It is one of the contradictions of Ralegh's personality
that while he himself knew what it was to be overweeningly
ambitious (and to be disappointed) his poems on the subject of
ambition are matchless.

Agnes Latham, Ralegh's editor, believes that this good-
humoured but cautionary poem was meant for Ralegh's elder
son, Walter, born in 1593, whom she describes as 'a wild young
spark'. As she says, neither the younger nor the elder Ralegh
ever needed to fear the rope: 'A gentleman claimed a right to the
axe.' But the poem is still an earnest one, even if it is based upon
an Elizabethan nursery-joke by which a little boy is threatened
with the gallows.

In order to understand this poem, which is a difficult one, it
is necessary to recognize from the outset that its tone is ironic.
We must imagine the speaker to be a man who has known mis-
fortune and bad luck; he is addressing people who share his kind

of experience, who are, so to speak, in the know about how hard and unfair life is. This is a matter of the tone, not of the meaning, as will become apparent when the poem has been fully assimilated.

The sense of the first four lines is perfectly clear. There are three things that quickly prosper when they are allowed to develop separately; but when they come together they affect each other for the worse. This seems to be an unexceptionable, innocent statement; it does nothing to prepare us for the shock of the last line. Only then may we go back to appreciate the bitter irony of line 3, with its bland sense of the inevitable, and the grim humour of line 4. The poem in fact works just as misfortune works in life: it comes suddenly upon us when we are not expecting it. Yet when we look back we may well discover that things apparently without significance at the time played their due part. Thus the poem presents a series of apparently innocuous statements, framed in a deliberately jocular way, and then springs a serious, even grim, surprise.

Lines 5–8 identify the three things that harm one another when they come together: they are the tree (the gallows), the weed (the hangman's rope) and the wag (again, a deliberately jocular term, meaning, of course, 'funny man; joker', and conveying the idea of a person who is happily unaware of his fate). The 'Hangmans bagg' is the hood that the hangman puts over the head of his victim, and the hemp is used to 'string' it.

Then in lines 9–12 the poet, again in a relaxed, jocular manner, asks the wag, the 'pritty knave', the 'deare boy', to note again that when these three things are separate, they prosper: the tree grows greenly, the grass (hemp) from which rope is made flourishes and the child is 'wilde', a word which suggests simultaneously 'heedless', 'dissolute in the manner of young men', and having the naturalness of wild things. The light-hearted tone is maintained in the last three lines; but the subject-matter suddenly becomes, one might say, disastrous. For the wag is to be hanged, for—we must presume—an excess of wildness, his heedlessness. These three things meet together only because of the dear boy's waggish notion that everything, including himself, will continue to flourish safely and separately. An old or dead tree was often chosen as a gallows, hence the rotting timber; 'it' in line 12 refers

to what happens when the three things meet. 'Frett' is a verb
meaning to 'chafe; rub; produce friction', a word whose applica-
tion to 'halter', the rope in which a man is hanged, is unpleasantly
obvious.

Why is this such an affecting poem? Mainly, there is no doubt,
because its extreme simplicity and gaiety—the gaiety of a man
lovingly admonishing his wild son, the same son who made his
tutor Ben Jonson drunk and 'caused him to be carried before
him on a shutter'—conceals a theme full of pathos: the innocent,
energetic heedlessness of the young is seen as tragically corrupting
nature itself, causing the green tree to rot into a gallows, the wild
hemp to turn into a halter, the boy into a horribly choked corpse.
And indeed, playful nursery threats (as Ralegh realized) do mask
real horrors. In his poem he succeeded perfectly in preserving a
loving tone, but at the same time remained true to what he knew
was the tragic irony of existence.

Winter is fallen early
On the house of Stare;
Birds in reverberating flocks
Haunt its ancestral box;
Bright are the plenteous berries   5
In clusters in the air.

Still is the fountain's music,
The dark pool icy still,
Whereupon a small and sanguine sun
Floats in a mirror on,   10
Into a West of crimson,
From a South of daffodil.

Tis strange to see young children
In such a wintry house;
Like rabbits' on the frozen snow   15
Their tell-tale footprints go;
Their laughter rings like timbrels
Neath evening ominous:

Their small and heightened faces
Like wine-red winter buds;   20
Their frolic bodies gentle as
Flakes in the air that pass,
Frail as the twirling petal
From the briar of the woods.

Above them silence lours,   25
Still as an arctic sea;
Light fails; night falls; the wintry moon
Glitters; the crocus soon
Will open grey and distracted
On earth's austerity: 30

Thick mystery, wild peril,
Law like an iron rod:—

Yet sport they on in Spring's attire,
        Each with his tiny fire
        Blown to a core of ardour   35
        By the awful breath of God.

Anyone at all familiar with the poems of Walter de la Mare would find little difficulty in identifying the author of this poem. First, the music reveals a superb ear. The poem should first be read aloud, without paying much attention to the sense. It should be read in grave and measured tones, nothing hurried. It seems that it has a magical quality in its language and music. Should this 'magic' be rejected? Let us see what is to be discovered.

Stanzas 1 and 2 describe the onset of winter upon the formal garden of an ancestral house. It is pretty certain that the name is fictional—atmospheric rather than actual. The fountain, either frozen or turned off, has filled a dark pool in which is reflected a vivid sunset. Stanza 3 describes children playing at dusk in the garden, running over the snow, laughing shrilly as they run. The last word of this stanza—'ominous'—sounds a new and, for the first time, not purely descriptive note. Why 'ominous'? In stanza 4 the children are described as 'gentle' and 'frail'. There is thus some hidden, some mysterious conflict between the frailty of the children and a threat from outer nature. In stanza 5 the laughter of the children is offset or opposed by a silence that 'lours'. Once again there is a hint of the ominous. Darkness is falling.

In stanza 6 de la Mare comes, as it were, more into the open. He speaks of 'Thick mystery, wild peril, / Law like an iron rod'. He is a poet of suggestion rather than statement. He does not hammer home his meaning or make it obvious. He writes for the reader who likes to read his own meaning into poetry, to some extent. No critic can be certain exactly what de la Mare intends by 'Thick mystery, wild peril, / Law like an iron rod'. What mystery, what peril, what law? Yet, the poet goes on, the children 'sport . . . on' in all the helplessness of youth, their small spirits made ardent by 'the . . . breath of God', the spark of divinity in each of them. It is reasonable to think that by 'mystery' and 'peril' de la Mare did not intend or wish to convey anything precise, and that by 'law with its iron rod' he meant, perhaps, not the laws of man and society but the laws of nature, by which they would grow old and die. This is, however, by no means certain, and it should be stressed that any attentive and sensitive reader is entitled to think otherwise.

De la Mare was not religious in any orthodox sense, and this is a religious poem only in the most general way. Nevertheless he expresses a belief in the essential divinity of innocent humanity in childhood, and the poem asserts, or rather represents, a sudden conviction of the frailty of young and innocent life amidst a threatening universe. The garden is not the whole world of the children; there are outer forces represented by the distant sunset, the approaching dark, the cold moon and the silence of night. Of these the children are unaware as they run laughing over the snow. Yet the poet, as he sees the children play, is aware of threatening forces, and it is this awareness, this sudden fear, that his poem expresses. What he is expressing is not an idea or a thought, but an intuition; and it is the business of the poem to objectify this intuition, as precisely as, but not more precisely than it can.

Many of de la Mare's poems have an at least partly literary inspiration. His deep reading of English poetry often reinforces his personal experience. A point worth considering is whether he owes anything in *The Children of Stare* to Gray's *Ode on a Distant Prospect of Eton College*:

> And there, regardless of their doom,
> The little victims play.

It is obvious that poets must often experience the same intuitions, and perhaps Gray and de la Mare were both struck, at different times, by a sense of the helplessness of children and their ignorance of the world they will soon enter. Each expressed his feeling in a totally different way. Yet the initial experience may have had something in common.

F

JOHN CROWE RANSOM: *Necrological*

The friar had said his paternosters duly
And scourged his limbs, and afterwards would have slept;
But with much riddling his head became unruly,
He arose, from the quiet monastery he crept.

Dawn lightened the place where the battle had been won.   5
The people were dead—it is easy he thought to die—
These dead remained, but the living all were gone,
Gone with the wailing trumps of victory.

The dead men wore no raiment against the air,
Bartholomew's men had spoiled them where they fell;   10
In defeat the heroes' bodies were whitely bare,
The field was white like meads of asphodel.

Not all were white; some gory and fabulous
Whom the sword had pierced and then the grey wolf eaten;
But the brother reasoned that heroes' flesh was thus,   15
Flesh fails, and the postured bones lie weather-beaten.

The lords of chivalry lay prone and shattered,
The gentle and the bodyguard of yeomen;
Bartholomew's stroke went home—but little it mattered,
Bartholomew went to be stricken of other foemen.   20

Beneath the blue ogive of the firmament
Was a dead warrior, clutching whose mighty knees
Was a leman, who with her flame had warmed his tent,
For him enduring all men's pleasantries.

Close by the sable stream that purged the plain   25
Lay the white stallion and his rider thrown,
The great beast had spilled there his little brain,
And the little groin of the knight was spilled by a stone.

The youth possessed him then of a crooked blade
Deep in the belly of a lugubrious wight;   30

74

He fingered it well, and it was cunningly made;
But strange apparatus was it for a Carmelite.

Then he sat upon a hill and hung his head,
Riddling, riddling, and lost in a vast surmise,
And so still that he likened himself unto those dead   35
Whom the kites of Heaven solicited with sweet cries.

This is a strange, difficult and tantalizing poem. Its atmosphere is
sombre and some of the details are gruesome. Its grave and formal
rhythm is appropriate to the seriousness of the subject. Its lan-
guage, very characteristic of Ransom, is at first sight odd, con-
taining as it does literary expressions ('the sable stream that
purged the plain'), archaisms ('leman', 'raiment'), semi-technical
terms ('ogive'—the shape of a Gothic arch) and words that are
unusual in their particular context ('fabulous', 'apparatus'). This
vocabulary has the effect of distancing the reader from the poem,
as if challenging him to make the effort to approach closer and
understand it on its own terms, as if to say 'These are not your
terms, but they are the only ones on which my meaning is to be
unriddled'. Moreover, although the poem deals with passion and
the issues of life and death, the treatment is cool and classical.
There is no romantic agony, no rhetorical or artificial heighten-
ing of tone. The language is precise, almost to the point of
pedantry. The poem evidently has something important to say.
    It is concerned with life and death. The title is quite deliber-
ately ambiguous, for 'necrology' has meant, over the centuries:
'an ecclesiastical register containing entries of the deaths of per-
sons connected with the church'; 'a death-roll' and 'an obituary
notice'. The adjective 'necrological' means 'obituary'. The prota-
gonist is a young friar (it is not till stanza 8 that he is called a
'youth') who is evidently a strict adherent of the Carmelite
Order. The Carmelites (in England 'White Friars' on account of
their habit) were eremitical, living in separate cells, devoting
themselves to prayer, silence, seclusion and abstinence. After
prayer and self-flagellation he tries to sleep, but his puzzled mind
will not let him. He goes out of the monastery to view the scene
of a battle which has just been fought. The sight of the dead

prompts him to the reflection 'It is easy . . . to die', implying that to live according to his vows is difficult. Bartholomew's men (there seems to be no special significance in the choice of a name) have been victorious, but it matters little whether in war one lives or dies. Death comes to all in the end. 'Heroes' flesh' is mortal. What matters is to have lived, to have spent one's strength in war or love. Under 'the blue ogive of the firmament' the knees of a dead, naked warrior are embraced by his mourning 'leman'—the mistress who had shared his tent and endured for his sake the ribaldries of the camp. There is a peculiar significance in the picture of heaven as an ogive, which suggests a Renaissance painting of the Madonna. It is as if the woman's devotion sanctifies her. There is another echo in the final line: the bodies of the heroes are the prey of the 'kites of Heaven'.

The sexual character of the friar's preoccupation is suggested in stanza 7. The dead rider (who must be the 'warrior' of stanza 6) has been dismembered by the fall, as his stallion has had its brains dashed out.

We are then told that the young friar does something 'strange' for a Carmelite: he possesses himself of a sharp knife. But what he wants it for we are not told. He does not know himself. He is left 'riddling' on a hillside with head downcast. If this suggests shame, or guilt, it must be because he is tempted either to kill or to castrate himself. This would be the only possible solution to the problem which is tormenting him—how to satisfy the needs of the flesh in the context of the monastic life. His flesh has not been assuaged by penance. The battle which chance has brought to the neighbourhood of the friary may, indeed, be seen as a symbol of his fever.

This is the nature of the riddle that torments the friar as his predicament is brought home all the more agonizingly by the contemplation of the field of battle. Victory and defeat are the same: flesh is mortal. Love and death are complementary aspects of living. The friar feels as if he were defeated, like the dead heroes. Only he and the warrior's mistress are alive on the battlefield. She stands for love and devotion to a man. The friar has only his devotion to heaven, and that is the home of birds of prey. He has, at least temporarily, lost his faith. So it is perhaps irrelevant to ask whether or not he makes use of the knife. The poem is neither a problem in mathematics nor a theological debate. It is a poem, aiming at the graphic presentation of a situation in which men have perennially found themselves. It stands or falls by the power of its imaginative treatment of a theme of universal interest.

23. TRUMBULL STICKNEY: *On some Shells found Inland*

These are my murmur-laden shells that keep
A fresh voice tho' the years be very gray.
The wave that washed their lips and tuned their lay
Is gone, gone with the faded ocean sweep,
The royal tide, gray ebb and sunken neap   5
And purple midday,—gone! To this hot clay
Must sing my shells, where yet the primal day,
Its roar and rhythm and splendour will not sleep.
What hand shall join them to their proper sea
If all be gone? Shall they forever feel   10
Glories undone and worlds that cannot be?—
'T were mercy to stamp out this agèd wrong,
Dash them to earth and crunch them with the heel
And make a dust of their seraphic song.

This is a poem ostensibly about what are called 'murmur-laden shells'—those in which you can hear a continuous, low, peaceful murmur by holding them to the ear. Owing to the recession of the sea, the shells have been found far inland, away from the ocean where their music properly belongs. In line 6 begins a passage of somewhat doubtful meaning. 'To this hot clay' (i.e. the land far from the sea) the shells must sing, 'where yet the primal day . . . will not sleep'. The poet seems here to be referring to himself, and it is clear by now that this is not simply a poem about shells. The poet's emotion is obviously too personal for that. It seems that, by listening to the shells inland, he is bringing to his ears the restless roar and rhythm of the distant 'royal' sea which has deserted the land. Must these shells, then, he asks, parted from their 'proper sea', 'feel / Glories undone and worlds that cannot be?' Better than that, he concludes, to crush the shells into the ground and put an end to their music.

The tone of the poem—its almost rhetorical passion, even anger—make it clear that Stickney is personally involved, that this is a statement of his own feelings and beliefs. He is overcome by a sense of frustration, of 'wrong'. The music he is writing of is removed from the original source of its inspiration, the sea. There is a gap which appears to the poet, in his hopelessness, unbridgeable.

Any poet must be concerned with his own mode of expression and of being. Clearly Stickney is thinking of poetry. This is thus a symbolist (see p. 84) poem in which an idea—the idea of poetic inspiration—is realized in concrete form as a passionate utterance about shells.

One point is not quite clear from the poem: is Stickney thinking of his own predicament as a poet, or is he thinking of the general situation of poetry in his time? Since any poet must to some extent equate his own predicament with that of poetry in general, the answer may be 'Both'.

To expand a little on this: Trumbull Stickney was an American poet writing at a time of extreme aridity in both American and English poetry. The great tide of Romanticism, which began in the eighteenth century and seemed to have achieved all it could by the fag-end of the nineteenth, when Stickney was writing, had ebbed and left the poet of genius and originality high and dry, like the shells found inland. So the shells evidently stand for two things: Stickney's own poetry and the poetry of the past, which he could hear but from which he felt helplessly alienated.

It would be worth discussing whether the poem is wholly successful, and whether allowance should be made for Stickney's youth. He died prematurely at the age of thirty, and was still experimenting when he died. The Keatsian extravagance of language which characterizes the poem shows that he had still not emancipated himself from Victorian influences. Nevertheless the genuine emotion, the sense of personal involvement, does make itself heard, and it is clear that this sonnet was no mere ninetyish exercise in a manner that was beginning to be outmoded.

No worst, there is none. Pitched past pitch of grief,
More pangs will, schooled at forepangs, wilder wring.
Comforter, where, where is your comforting?
Mary, mother of us, where is your relief?
My cries heave, herds-long; huddle in a main, a chief   5
Woe, wórld-sorrow; on an áge-old anvil wince and sing—
Then lull, then leave off. Fury had shrieked 'No ling-
ering! Let me be fell: force I must be brief'.

O the mind, mind has mountains; cliffs of fall
Frightful, sheer, no-man-fathomed. Hold them cheap   10
May who ne'er hung there. Nor does long our small
Durance deal with that steep or deep. Here! creep,
Wretch, under a comfort serves in a whirlwind: all
Life death does end and each day dies with sleep.

Gerard Manley Hopkins (1844–89) was born out of his time.
Only a handful of his poems were printed in the nineteenth
century, since his friend and mentor Robert Bridges, later Poet
Laureate, did not feel them technically or even emotionally suit-
able for the times. His poems were eventually issued by Bridges
in 1918. This Victorian poet has influenced and is still influencing
the development of English poetry to as great a degree as Ezra
Pound, T. S. Eliot or W. B. Yeats. Hopkins was a Jesuit priest
and teacher who partially shared the official view of his Order
that the writing of poetry might well be regarded as a terrible
self-indulgence—an expression, perhaps, of things about the self
that were better left to God, and not dwelt upon. Only his close
friend Canon R. W. Dixon, himself a graceful minor poet, showed
Hopkins any real comprehension or sympathy during his life-
time, although Bridges, a vastly inferior poet, did his best.
Hopkins lived a difficult, piously devoted, unhappy life, subject
to moods of elation (about which he suffered theological guilt)
followed by depression. This sonnet is one of a series he wrote in
1885 justifiably known as 'the terrible sonnets'. These have been

called 'the uncensored expression of Hopkins' naked soul'.* They
are full of daring linguistic innovations, which make them hard to
read, and yet in a way their subject is simple: for in them Hopkins,
in a mood of black depression, is facing utter despair; his alter-
natives are death or madness. All this comes out starkly in the
unusual word-order, the strangely effective breaking of words in
the middle (thus the violent enjambement 'ling-ering' in lines 7/8
adds agony to the sense of the word by prolonging it), and the
rhythms, which seem to bodily assault the conventional metrical
structure, and yet which possess a vitality and an energy that
seem to challenge the sombre mood of the poem. This sonnet
needs first to be read aloud, with every allowance made for
Hopkins' passionate grief. Then, soaked in its mood, perhaps
recollecting occasions when we, too, have been assailed by black
depression or despair, we may proceed to an exegesis.

The first sentence states the theme: 'there is no bottom limit
to this suffering.' The poem is remarkable in that it deals solely
with, and painfully analyses, the state of mental suffering; the
reason for this suffering only emerges later. (Indeed, Hopkins'
particular suffering was probably of the sort called endogenous
—that is, coming from within himself, originating in internal
conflicts, not actuated by exterior circumstances; but readers can
discover that this poem applies to any real suffering.)

The next sentence is difficult, an astonishingly precise analysis
of the actual processes of grief or depression. 'Pitched' here com-
bines its senses of (i) 'to place'; 'throw'; 'cast' and (ii) the musical
sense of 'to determine the pitch of' (Hopkins was a practising
composer of music); the word also means, of course, blackness.
This suggests the high-pitched shrieks of a suffering person, a
motif which is taken up again in line 5.

The complicated sense of the whole sentence is: 'Those violent
convulsions of grief that may seem to offer some temporary relief
to the sufferer by actually, with the pain they cause, distracting
him from his central despair, will, by association with earlier con-
vulsions ("schooled at forepangs") produce an extra agony.'

We can now see with what justice this poem is known as

* James Reeves, Introduction to *Selected Poems of Gerard Manley
Hopkins*, xxv.

'terrible'. The subject-matter is morbid, yes; but the poem carries us beyond morbidity and self-pity by the piercing accuracy of its analysis—an accuracy earned by the poet's having gone the whole way with his grief, by his devotion to truth. The impotent 'Comforter' of line 3 may refer, for the reader, to any figure who familiarly offers comfort; in Hopkins' case, it undoubtedly refers to the Holy Ghost, and it parallels the words of Christ on the cross, 'Eli, Eli, Lama Sabachtani', 'O Lord, Lord, Why hast thou forsaken me?' That Hopkins meant this is made apparent by the next line, a direct appeal to the Virgin Mary.

The following lines continue the description and analysis of the actual processes of naked grief. 'My cries heave' means that his cries 'swell up', with perhaps a suggestion of the semi-nautical sense of 'hauling', as if with an agonizing effort; 'herds-long' means that his cries follow one another stretched out like cattle in a herd. The next phrase, 'huddle in a main', describes a new process, for this sonnet is never static—it is always moving, charting the dynamics of grief. The word 'main', used here as a noun, combines the senses of 'a broad expanse', and 'the most important part'; 'huddle' means not only 'to crowd together' but also 'to drive hurriedly': in other words, the difficult sense of the first two lines is recalled: his cries, stretched out, suddenly crowd together, to add up to a 'chief woe', a 'world-sorrow' (this is really an Anglicizing of the useful German word *Weltschmerz*, used to signify a cosmic as opposed to a personal grief). The poet's pain is 'age-old': whatever had caused it, it is now a universal grief for original sin: the wickedness not only of himself but also of all men. The last two lines of the octave (as the first, eight-line section of a sonnet is called) state that 'Fury' had insisted that there should be no lingering: 'I must be terrible, destructive, dire ("fell")', the poet makes 'Fury' say, 'I must of necessity ("force", meaning "perforce") by brief, quick, killing.' This 'Fury' may be understood not only as Hopkins' personal Catholic God of Righteousness, but also as the power of truth speaking in wrath, stating that it must destroy because of the evil that is in the sufferer. It has brought this grief to a head, even forced the sufferer to confront his absolute pain, rather than to indulge himself in 'pangs', 'schooled at forepangs'.

The sestet, the concluding six-line section of the sonnet, is a quieter comment on the octave. The mind, it states, has 'mountains': we can drop from euphoria—well-being, ecstasy—to despair in an instant ('cliffs of fall / Frightful'); but no one has explored the utter depths. People who have not experienced this kind of despair may sneer ('Hold them cheap / May who ne'er hung there'); but in any case not even those who have are long able to withstand the anguish of absolute despair ('Nor does long our small / Durance deal with that steep or deep'). In other words, in the face of this 'Fury' who so terribly insists upon concentrating our grief, there is only death, madness—or poetry. For the poem is in itself an alternative to these two alternatives. And it ends by despairingly inviting the sufferer to sleep. 'Here! creep / Wretch' is, however, partly an invitation to enter the poem, a temporary answer, like sleep; 'under a comfort serves in a whirlwind' is an almost demotic, proverbial way of saying 'anything will do to shelter you from trouble when you're in it'. You can kill grief with sleep: in the same way as death ends life, sleep ends the painful day. But there is an irony here that makes the poem yet more 'terrible'. For the poet, by his reference to Mary in line 4 (apart from what else we know about him: that he was a most sincere and pious Jesuit priest) does not believe that death 'ends' real life. He is afraid, because of the evil in him (which is the cause of his grief), of the final judgement of death. From sleep we must awake to another day; from the death that we glibly say ends life we must awake to another, perhaps terrible, life in hell. Compare this poem with *The Pains of Sleep* (p. 148).

25. WALLACE STEVENS: *The Emperor of Ice-Cream*

Call the roller of big cigars,
The muscular one, and bid him whip
In kitchen cups concupiscent curds.
Let the wenches dawdle in such dress
As they are used to wear, and let the boys   5
Bring flowers in last month's newspapers.
Let be be finale of seem.
The only emperor is the emperor of ice-cream.

Take from the dresser of deal,
Lacking the three glass knobs, that sheet   10
On which she embroidered fantails once
And spread it so as to cover her face.
If her horny feet protrude, they come
To show how cold she is, and dumb.
Let the lamp affix its beam.   15
The only emperor is the emperor of ice-cream.

This is a difficult, and at first sight even incoherent poem. Is it better to enjoy its surface attractiveness—the bizarre, but clear-cut imagery—or should the reader make a serious attempt to get inside it? As with many modern poems, there are a number of possible approaches to it. While it has its own vitality, a kind of exuberant self-confidence on the part of the poet, which answers, or partially answers, the objection that it is incoherent, it may be considered as either a symbolist poem, where each object stands for something else, or as a reversion, in adult sophisticated terms, to the kind of childhood material that is found in nursery rhymes.

Is another answer to the objection that this poem is 'meaning-less' that the objector never pauses to make the same kind of accusations against nursery rhymes or against, for example, *Alice in Wonderland*?

The following interpretation is an attempt to get inside the poem: it does not rely upon any theory of interpretation, e.g. the 'symbolist' or the 'nonsense' theory; rather, it makes use of every clue the poem itself affords.

Is such an interpretation of any help to the reader? Does it lead him back to the poem itself, or only into the mind of the critic? Before reading this account, re-read the poem with special concentration, to see what you can make of it.

This is a poem not of direct logical statement, but of concrete visual imagery. Only lines 7, 8, 15 (and 16) are apparently non-visual; and of these the repeated line, 'The only emperor is the emperor of ice-cream', at least conjures up a kind of picture as well as making a humorously dogmatic statement. Line 15 depends on a visual image if sense is to be made of it. This leaves us with line 7, 'Let be be finale of seem', which because it is the only strictly non-visual line in the poem may therefore have a special significance.

The poem is in some way about childhood: its total lack of formal logic, together with the reference to the only emperor being the emperor of ice-cream, makes this evident. Now the age—if we remember our own experience—when ice-cream is really important, a placatory treat having emotional as well as gustatory significance, is round about two to five. The significance ice-cream originally has in our lives is as a token of love and reassurance which is also nice to eat; by the parent it is regarded as delicious, a treat, an offering to the loved infant; consequently the loved infant soon learns to regard it in a similar light. Deprived of the ice-cream he howls and feels deprived also of love and of pleasure. It, and of course all it stands for, is his only 'emperor'.

No infant, however, could think in the terms of this poem, which is self-consciously elegant, learned ('concupiscent curds' is obviously a 'clever' phrase) and humorous. Thus, it must be taken to be an adult version of a child's consciousness; a memory of innocence, illogicality and infantile egotism that is made nostalgic because it is so sophisticated.

The 'roller of big cigars' is father, who, in whipping up the 'concupiscent curds' is making ice-cream for the child. As we shall see in the next stanza, the mother has just died. This way of regarding the poem is reinforced by the pun on 'ice-cream': 'I scream'. For the child *screams* if he is deprived of ice-cream, love or attention; and, of course, in order to assert himself or get his own way (be an 'emperor') he is obliged to scream.

The poem does not simply consist of a series of statements. It consists of a series of imperatives (note that emperor (imperator) is the one who gives commands): (1) an imperative (lines 1–6); (2) another imperative (line 7); (3) a statement (line 8), which may, as we shall see, help to explain the nature of the imperatives; (4) a third imperative (lines 9–12); (5) a statement based on a possibility arising from the imperative expressed in (4) (lines 13–14); (6) a fourth imperative (line 15); (7) a repetition of the first statement (line 16).

These imperatives must be regarded not as the infant himself thinking (or commanding)—for, as we have noted, infants do not have this capacity for conceptual thought—but as the self-indulgent projections of the sophisticated, not innocent, poet, who knows more than the infant, and can be nicely bluff (as in line 1) about what infants like. There is an almost parodic element in these utterances: an element that by parodying adult self-indulgence emphasizes the actual, tragic distance between the man and the child he was—tragic because of the loss of innocence as well as the closer proximity of death.

The infant is represented as desiring, first of all, fun: the father-figure of the burly roller of huge cigars, who is now to be ordered, grotesquely, to whip up lustful curds (ice-cream) in cups. It is the sophisticated word 'concupiscent', denoting lust and greed for the things of the world, that most sharply emphasizes that this account of an episode of infantile egoism is parodic and regretful. The next two lines bring together memories of things vividly present to the eye of the child on the occasion of his mother's death, but add adult knowledge: the tone of 'As they are used to wear' and the information that the newspapers are old, are wholly adult.

Then comes the second, suddenly abstract, imperative: 'Let be be finale of seem'. This has a dual function: first, it is the fervent wish, on the part of the adult who is vainly attempting to imitate the infant's innocent—if egoistic—way of experiencing, to be able really to enter into his state of mind and therefore into a state of innocence; secondly, it sums up the infant's own, possibly tragic, state of mind: 'let this be real; let innocence actually exist coherently; let me be able to articulate my lovely drollness, my innocence; let reality replace this illusion'.

But, for the infant, the only emperor is the emperor of ice-cream ('I scream'), and for the adult vainly imitating him, attempting to enter his innocence, the only emperor is the emperor of 'I scream' (with desperation and horror), of placatory, silly, ineffective symbolic-of-our-kitch age ice-cream.

The sexual overtones of the first stanza, 'big cigar', 'concupiscent', 'wenches', not only help to emphasize the impossible distance between adulthood and childhood, but also lead to the murderous, perhaps necrophilic impulses that are expressed in the second stanza.

Here, the viciousness of the performance by which adulthood imitates childhood becomes explicit: the 'ice-cream' of line 8 becomes in line 16 an unequivocal 'I scream', and it is printed as 'ice-cream' only because such murderous situations are masked ludicrously, by mundaneness, by ordinariness. For the 'she' of line 11 must refer to the infant's mother—the most important 'she' in any infant's life; and she is grotesquely dead. It thus emerges that the poem is, in its comically oblique way, dealing with a father–child situation (the sex of the infant is not made explicit). There may be a reference, conscious or unconscious, to the familiar Freudian Oedipus situation, in which it is postulated that every son wishes to murder his father and enjoy his mother. The father has, dangerously, tried to enter into his child's world; the result is that the to-be-ravished mother is now dead, must be covered with the sheet upon which once she embroidered pigeons. She is cold and dumb.

The speaker of the poem, the imitator of the child, has violated the instinctive mother–child relationship by his intellectuality— for intellectuality, the triumph and the defeat of man, is what a man has and animals have not; but it can cruelly deny the instincts within ourselves that are animal.

Then comes the most difficult line in the poem, 'Let the lamp affix its beam'. Affix its beam to what ('affix' simply means 'attach')? The only possible interpretation involves suggesting that the verb 'affix' is not used very precisely here: the line seems to mean, 'Let the lamp fix its beam to shine in one direction only', to intend a more visual metaphor for 'Let be be finale of seem': 'Let the shifting lamp stop making things appear ambiguous, and concentrate its light upon one area, or in one direction'.

This interpretation is offered not as definitive, but as an example of one means of getting inside an admittedly difficult poem. Does it help or hinder the reader? Is it over-ingenious? Is the use of Freudian concepts, so common in modern criticism, relevant? What image in the second stanza conveys most vividly the exactness and purity of a child's vision?

Part II

Part II

26. JOHN CLARE: *Badger*

When midnight comes a host of dogs and men
Go out and track the badger to his den,
And put a sack within the hole, and lie
Till the old grunting badger passes by.
He comes and hears—they let the strongest loose.   5
The old fox hears the noise and drops the goose.
The poacher shoots and hurries from the cry,
And the old hare half wounded buzzes by.
They get a forkèd stick to bear him down
And clap the dogs and take him to the town,   10
And bait him all the day with many dogs,
And laugh and shout and fright the scampering hogs.
He runs along and bites at all he meets:
They shout and hollo down the noisy streets.
He turns about to face the loud uproar   15
And drives the rebels to their very door.
And frequent stone is hurled where'er they go;
When badgers fight, then every one's a foe.
The dogs are clapt and urged to join the fray;
The badger turns and drives them all away.   20
Though scarcely half as big, demure and small,
He fights with dogs for hours and beats them all.
The heavy mastiff, savage in the fray,
Lies down and licks his feet and turns away.
The bulldog knows his match and waxes cold,   25
The badger grins and never leaves his hold.
He drives the crowd and follows at their heels
And bites them through—the drunkard swears and reels.
The frighted women take the boys away,
The blackguard laughs and hurries on the fray.   30
He tries to reach the woods, an awkward race,
But sticks and cudgels quickly stop the chase.
He turns agen and drives the noisy crowd
And beats the many dogs in noises loud.
He drives away and beats them every one,   35
And then they loose them all and set them on.
He falls as dead and kicked by boys and men,

Then starts and grins and drives the crowd agen;
Till kicked and torn and beaten out he lies
And leaves his hold and cackles, groans, and dries.   40

1. Name three nocturnal creatures who are disturbed by the arrival of the men and dogs.
2. What line in the poem has the ring of a country proverb?
3. What people in the town are mentioned as being disturbed by the hunt in the streets?
4. What is the effect of the two epithets 'demure' and 'heavy'?
5. 'Bulldog', 'blackguard' and 'drunkard' are mentioned without any descriptive epithets. Would the poem have been improved by the addition of epithets?
6. This poem appears at first to be purely descriptive or narrative —a factual account of a badger hunt. Do you think that there is any evidence of personal feeling about the hunt?
7. By what means does Clare stress the fact that he is describing a fight by one against many?
8. By what means does Clare keep up the pace of the narrative?
9. Why does the fight have to start at midnight?
10. Clare often felt that, as a poet among country labourers, he was 'odd man out' in the Northampton village where he lived. Is there a case to be made out for saying that, in this poem, he identifies himself with the hunted creature?
11. Does Clare moralize about the hunt? Would this poem be suitable as propaganda for the RSPCA?
12. The badger hunt about the turn of the eighteenth century was one country pastime giving scope for working off feelings of aggression or an instinct for violent action. What substitutes for such a hunt have been found since that time?

27. EDWARD LEAR: *The Dong with a Luminous Nose*

When awful darkness and silence reign
Over the great Gromboolian plain,
   Through the long, long wintry nights;—
    When the angry breakers roar
    As they beat on the rocky shore;—   5
When Storm-clouds brood on the towering heights
    Of the Hills of the Chankly Bore:—

Then, through the vast and gloomy dark,
There moves what seems a fiery spark,
   A lonely spark with silvery rays   10
    Piercing the coal-black night,—
    A meteor strange and bright;—
Hither and thither the vision strays,
    A single lurid light.

Slowly it wanders,—pauses,—creeps,—   15
Anon it sparkles,—flashes and leaps;
And ever as onward it gleaming goes
A light on the Bong-tree stems it throws.

And those who watch at that midnight hour
From Hall or Terrace, or lofty Tower,   20
Cry, as the wild light passes along,—
    'The Dong!—the Dong!
  The wandering Dong through the forest goes!
    The Dong!—the Dong!
  The Dong with a luminous Nose!'   25

    Long years ago
   The Dong was happy and gay,
Till he fell in love with a Jumbly Girl
  Who came to those shores one day.
For the Jumblies came in a Sieve, they did,—   30
Landing at eve near the Zemmery Fidd
    Where the Oblong Oysters grow,
  And the rocks are smooth and gray.

And all the woods and valleys rang
With the Chorus they daily and nightly sang,— 35
    'Far and few, far and few,
    Are the lands where the Jumblies live;
    Their heads are green, and their hands are blue,
    And they went to sea in a sieve.'

Happily, happily passed those days! 40
    While the cheerful Jumblies staid;
  They danced in circles all night long,
  To the plaintive pipe of the lively Dong,
    In moonlight, shine or shade.
For day and night he was always there 45
By the side of the Jumbly Girl so fair,
With her sky-blue hands, and her sea-green hair.

Till the morning came of that hateful day
When the Jumblies sailed in their sieve away,
And the Dong was left on the cruel shore 50
Gazing—gazing for evermore,—
Ever keeping his weary eyes on
That pea-green sail on the far horizon,—
Singing the Jumbly Chorus still
As he sate all day on the grassy hill,— 55
    'Far and few, far and few,
    Are the lands where the Jumblies live;
    Their heads are green, and their hands are blue,
    And they went to sea in a sieve.'

But when the sun was low in the West, 60
    The Dong arose and said,—
    'What little sense I once possessed
  Has quite gone out of my head!'
And since that day he wanders still
By lake and forest, marsh and hill, 65
Singing—'O somewhere, in valley or plain
Might I find my Jumbly Girl again!
For ever I'll seek by lake and shore
Till I find my Jumbly Girl once more!'

Playing a pipe with silvery squeaks,   70
Since then his Jumbly Girl he seeks.
And because by night he could not see,
He gathered the bark of the Twangum Tree
    On the flowery plain that grows.
    And he wove him a wondrous Nose,—   75
A Nose as strange as a Nose could be!
Of vast proportions and painted red,
And tied with cords to the back of his head.
    —In a hollow rounded space it ended
    With a luminous lamp within suspended,   80
      All fenced about
      With a bandage stout
      To prevent the wind from blowing it out;—
And with holes all round to send the light,
In gleaming rays on the dismal night.   85

And now each night, and all night long,
Over those plains still roams the Dong;
And above the wail of the Chimp and Snipe
You may hear the squeak of his plaintive pipe
While ever he seeks, but seeks in vain   90
To meet with his Jumbly Girl again;
Lonely and wild—all night he goes—
The Dong with a luminous Nose.
And all who watch at the midnight hour,
From Hall or Terrace, or lofty Tower,   95
Cry, as they trace the Meteor bright,
Moving along through the dreary night,—
    'This is the hour when forth he goes,
    The Dong with a luminous Nose!
    Yonder—over the plain he goes;   100
      He goes!
      He goes!
    The Dong with a luminous Nose!'

1. 'The Chankly Bore', 'the Zemmery Fidd', 'the great Gromboolian plain'—are these real or imaginary places? What continent would they be likely to be located in? What effect is Lear trying to produce by naming them?

2. Can you visualize the Dong? Are you intended to have any precise picture of him, apart from his nose? By what strokes does Lear make the description of the nose graphic?

3. The Dong—subject of the poem—is not mentioned till stanza 4. What is the effect of the first three stanzas? How do the words 'awful', 'angry', 'brood' and 'lurid' contribute to this effect?

4. The Dong, after the departure of the Jumblies, admits that he is out of his mind. Is he right? Why?

5. Why does the Dong fashion and wear his strange nose?

6. By what single word does Lear indicate the temperament (*not* the appearance) of the Jumblies? In what way, other than the disappearance of the Jumbly girl of his choice, would the Dong find life different after they had gone?

7. The vividness of the poem depends on Lear's use of imagery—visual and aural. What words indicating sound does he employ most effectively?

8. Quote three or four examples of alliteration. What is their effect?

9. Apart from the Jumbly chorus, one couplet in the poem is repeated. Which is it? What is the purpose of its vagueness?

10. Does this poem require a musical setting, or is its own verbal music enough?

11. What earlier poets does it remind you of? Is the poem purely a parody? Is it correctly described by Lear's own word—'Nonsense'? What function had 'nonsense' in the mid-Victorian age?

12. Has it a function now?

13. Is the poem wholly frivolous?

14. Is the final effect of the poem one of humour, pathos or what? Is Lear simply parodying Victorian poems about blighted romantic love, or is there more to this poem?

15. How would you answer a critic who described *The Dong with a Luminous Nose* as nothing but rubbish?

16. Is the poem worthy of notice by adults, or is it simply verse for children? What other adult works have made their first impact on children?

17. Do you think the poem has any autobiographical significance?

28. THOMAS HARDY: *Friends Beyond*

William Dewy, Tranter Reuben, Farmer Ledlow late at plough,
    Robert's kin, and John's and Ned's,
And the Squire, and Lady Susan, lie in Mellstock churchyard
    now!

'Gone,' I call them, gone for good, that group of local hearts
    and heads;
    Yet at mothy curfew-tide,   5
And at midnight when the noon-heat breathes it back from
    walls and leads,

They've a way of whispering to me—a fellow-wight who yet
    abide—
    In the muted, measured note
Of a ripple under archways, or a lone cave's stillicide:

'We have triumphed: this achievement turns the bane to
    antidote,   10
    Unsuccesses to success,
Many thought-worn eves and morrows to a morrow free of
    thought.

'No more need we corn and clothing, feel of old terrestrial
    stress;
    Chill detraction stirs no sigh;
Fear of death has even bygone us: death gave all that we
    possess.'   15

W.D.—'Ye mid burn the old bass-viol that I set such value
    by.'
Squire.—'You may hold the manse in fee,
    You may wed my spouse, may let my children's memory
    of me die.'

Lady S.—'You may have my rich brocades, my laces; take
    each household key;
    Ransack coffer, desk, bureau;   20

Quiz the few poor treasures hid there, con the letters
  kept by me.'

Far.—'Ye mid zell my favourite heifer, ye mid let the
  charlock grow,
    Foul the grinterns, give up thrift.'
Far. Wife.—'If ye break my best blue china, children, I
  shan't care or ho.'

All.—'We've no wish to hear the tidings, how the people's
  fortunes shift;   25
    What your daily doings are;
  Who are wedded, born, divided; if your lives beat slow
    or swift.'

'Curious not the least are we if our intents you make or mar,
    If you quire to our old tune,
  If the City stage still passes, if the weirs still roar afar.'   30

—Thus, with very gods' composure, freed those crosses late
  and soon
    Which, in life, the Trine allow
(Why, none witteth), and ignoring all that haps beneath the
  moon,

William Dewy, Tranter Reuben, Farmer Ledlow late at plough,
    Robert's kin, and John's and Ned's,   35
  And the Squire, and Lady Susan, murmur mildly to me now.

Tranter   carrier
leads   flat leaded roofs
stillicide   dripping of water from roofs of caves to form stalag-
mites and stalactites
hold the manse in fee   have absolute possession of the manor
charlock   mustard
grinterns   compartments in a granary
ho   worry
Trine   Trinity

1. In what stanza does the poet hint that he is spoken to by the
ghosts of the dead?

2. In what phrase does he speak of himself as the only one of the local group who remains alive?

3. If you read the poem slowly and regularly, pausing at the ends of lines, does its rhythm remind you of any rhythmic happening mentioned in the poem?

4. 'We have triumphed . . .': in what has death brought the group triumph? Is it real triumph? Which words are ironic?

5. Read for comparison Shakespeare's *Dirge* in *Cymbeline* ('Fear no more the heat o' the sun'). What phrases in stanza 5 of Hardy's poem recall Shakespeare's?

6. In which stanza does the poet refer to the neighbourly chat and gossip which make much of village life and intercourse?

7. Which of the speakers, when alive, was interested in family pride? Which valued privacy? Which played music?

8. If Lady Susan was the Squire's wife, which of the two died first?

9. There is no stanza allotted to Tranter Reuben. Compose a stanza in the same form and metre suitable to Reuben.

10. Is the attitude of the dead people one of bitterness? indignation? joy? resignation? indifference? hope of an eternal life?

11. Would you call the poem religious?

12. Are the ghosts speaking to Hardy, or is the poet putting words into their mouths?

13. What evidence is there of class distinction in the words of the various speakers?

14. Compare this poem with Clare's *Country Letter* (p. 13). Which poem represents country speech more naturally?

15. The poem is mainly factual and speculative, but there are some vivid, characteristic descriptive phrases. Which do you consider the most striking?

16. Is the attitude of the poet to the 'friends beyond' one of love? indifference? pity? envy? regret?

29. CONRAD AIKEN: *The Nameless Ones*

Pity the nameless, and the unknown, where
bitter in heart they wait on the stonebuilt stair,
bend to a wall, forgotten, the freezing wind
no bitterer than the suburbs of the mind;

who from an iron porch lift sightless eyes, 5
a moment, hopeless, to inflaming skies;
shrink from the light as quickly as from pain,
twist round a corner, bend to the wall again;

are to be seen leaning against a rail
by ornamental waters where toy yachts sail; 10
glide down the granite steps, touch foot to float,
hate, and desire, the sunlight on the boat;

explore a sullen alley where ash-cans wait,
symbols of waste and want, at every gate;
emerge in sun to mingle with the crowd, 15
themselves most silent where the world most loud;

anonymous, furtive, shadows in shadow hidden;
who lurk at the garden's edge like guests unbidden;
stare through the leaves with hate, yet wait to listen
as bandstand music begins to rise and glisten; 20

the fierce, the solitary, divine of heart,
passionate, present, yet godlike and apart;
who, in the midst of traffic, see a vision;
and, on a park bench, come to a last decision.

1. Which line in the poem most strikingly suggests bitterness?
2. Why do some of the nameless 'shrink from the light? (line 7).
3. What do you take 'the suburbs of the mind' (line 4) to mean?
4. Why are ashcans called 'symbols of waste and want' (line 14)?
5. In what way are the nameless in the final stanza different from those previously mentioned?

6. Are we told the nature of the 'last decision' referred to in the final line? What do you think it might be?

7. There is one verb used in the imperative mood. What is it? Why does the poet use this mood?

8. What word in the poem is synonymous with the epithet in the title?

9. Mention two similes or comparisons. What, in each case, is the effect?

10. In line 2 'stonebuilt' suggests a cold hardness and so enhances the effect of the poem by its association with the state of mind of the nameless. Mention three other nouns or adjectives having a similar effect but not applied directly to the nameless.

11. What is the effect of the metaphor 'glisten' in line 20?

12. Every line rhymes: the poem is in rhymed couplets. One of the difficulties of sustaining this scheme is that word-order tends to be inverted on occasion, to accommodate a rhyme. Does Aiken avoid this? Give examples to illustrate your answer.

13. The rhymed couplets are not rhythmically regular like those of an Augustan poet. Point out three or four irregular lines. Is the effect less or more pleasing than would be the effect of strict regularity? Why?

14. One line in the poem has the rhythmical regularity and antithetical balance of an Augustan line. Which is it?

15. What is the purpose of the rhymes? Would the poem have been as effective if there had been no rhymes?

16. Aiken is an American and wrote this poem a good many years ago, possibly in America. Where might a similar kind of experience be found in Britain today?

17. If you had not been given Aiken's title, what title would you have suggested?

18. Can this poem be regarded as propaganda? Was it so intended? How high do you rate it?

19. Write a poem in this metre, rhymed or unrhymed, or in free verse, entitled either 'At a Football Ground', 'In a Railway Station' or 'Demonstration'.

30. EDMUND BLUNDEN: *The Ballast-Hole*

Can malice live in natural forms,
As tree, or stone, or winding lane?
Beside this winding lane of ours
The fangy roots of trees contain
A pond that seems to feed the powers   5
Of ugly passion. Thunder-storms
No blacker look. If forth it shook
Blue snarling flashes lightning-like,
I scarce should marvel; may it strike
When I'm not by its sullen dyke!   10

A ballast-hole is a hole left when sand or gravel has been excavated.

1. What does the poet mean by his first question? Does the poem answer this question in the negative or the affirmative?
2. What words and phrases in the poem does the writer use to emphasize his view about malice in nature?
3. What reason does the poet give for his statement that the pond 'seems to feed the powers / Of ugly passion'?
4. What surrounds the pond? What adjective makes these surroundings seem sinister or threatening? Why?
5. What action might the pond perform that would not amaze the poet? What does he hope in connection with this?
6. Describe in as much detail as you can how the poet answers his opening question. How does one statement develop from the other?
7. Taking 'archaism' to mean 'any expression which is not contemporary', are there any archaisms in the poem—in the form of words or word-order?
8. Say why you think this is an effective—or an ineffective—poem. Write your own short description, in verse, or in prose if you wish, of some object that strikes you as having the same kind of unhappy or happy or sinister or joyful associations as Blunden's little pond had for him.

The man Flammonde, from God knows where,
With firm address and foreign air,
With news of nations in his talk
And something royal in his walk,
With glint of iron in his eyes,   5
But never doubt, nor yet surprise,
Appeared, and stayed, and held his head
As one by kings accredited.

Erect, with his alert repose
About him, and about his clothes,   10
He pictured all tradition hears
Of what we owe to fifty years.
His cleansing heritage of taste
Paraded neither want nor waste;
And what he needed for his fee   15
To live, he borrowed graciously.

He never told us what he was,
Or what mischance, or other cause,
Had banished him from better days
To play the Prince of Castaways.   20
Meanwhile he played surpassing well
A part, for most, unplayable;
In fine, one pauses, half afraid
To say for certain that he played.

For that, one may as well forego   25
Conviction as to yes or no;
Nor can I say just how intense
Would then have been the difference
To several, who, having striven
In vain to get what he was given   30
Would see the stranger taken on
By friends not easy to be won.

Moreover, many a malcontent
He soothed and found munificent;
His courtesy beguiled and foiled   35
Suspicion that his years were soiled;
His mien distinguished any crowd,
His credit strengthened when he bowed;
And women, young and old, were fond
Of looking at the man Flammonde.   40

There was a woman in our town
On whom the fashion was to frown;
But while our talk renewed the tinge
Of a long-faced scarlet fringe,
The man Flammonde saw none of that,   45
And what he saw we wondered at—
That none of us, in her distress,
Could hide or find our littleness.

There was a boy that all agreed
Had shut within him the rare seed   50
Of learning. We could understand,
But none of us could lift a hand.
The man Flammonde appraised the youth,
And told a few of us the truth;
And thereby, for a little gold,   55
A flowered future was unrolled.

There were two citizens who fought
For years and years, and over nought;
They made life awkward for their friends,
And shortened their own dividends.   60
The man Flammonde said what was wrong
Should be made right; nor was it long
Before they were again in line,
And had each other in to dine.

And these I mention are but four   65
Of many out of many more.
So much for them. But what of him—
So firm in every look and limb?

What small satanic sort of kink
Was in his brain? What broken link   70
Withheld him from the destinies
That came so near to being his?

What was he, when we came to sift
His meaning, and to note the drift
Of incommunicable ways   75
That make us ponder while we praise?
Why was it that this charm revealed
Somehow the surface of a shield?
What was it that we never caught?
What was he, and what was he not?   80

How much it was of him we met
We cannot ever know; nor yet
Shall all he gave us quite atone
For what was his, and his alone;
Nor need we now, since he knew best,   85
Nourish an ethical unrest:
Rarely at once will nature give
The power to be Flammonde and live.

We cannot know how much we learn
From those who never will return,   90
Until a flash of unforeseen
Remembrance falls on what has been.
We've each a darkening hill to climb;
And this is why, from time to time
In Tilbury Town, we look beyond   95
Horizons for the man Flammonde.

Flammonde appears in the volume *The Man Against the Sky*
(1916), by which the American Edwin Arlington Robinson
(1869–1935) gained recognition as a poet. 'Tilbury Town', of
this and many other of his best poems, was his name for Gar-
diner, Maine, where he grew up. Robinson, whose long struggle
to establish himself as a poet was bitter, fierce and fortified by
courage and alcohol, employed traditional forms but was ahead
of his time in his rejection of Victorian sentimentality. When he

H

sent his first, privately printed volume, *The Torrent and the Night Before* (1896), to Thomas Hardy he received an appreciative reply.

Flammonde is a highly characteristic poem. Set in 'Tilbury Town', it presents a complete psychological portrait of a man in dramatic form. It holds the reader's attention by being not too simple: by posing the sort of enigmas that people themselves pose. A debt to Browning is discernible; but Robinson's intuitive method of psychological analysis is very much his own. Note the care with which he builds up the picture of Flammonde, adding subtle touch to subtle touch: this in itself amounts to a rejection of the evil small-town pseudo-morality that judges a man or woman by one or two facets of his or her character or by a single manifestation of his or her personality. In fact people are extremely complicated, as this poem truthfully demonstrates.

1. Give from stanza 1 three features of the man Flammonde that show he was a stranger to 'Tilbury Town'.
2. Why should a man who comes 'from God knows where' be suggested as picturing 'all tradition hears / Of what we owe to fifty years'?
3. At what point in the first 3 stanzas does the author introduce a note of ironic reserve on the matter of Flammonde's character?
4. What may we learn, from the same initial passage, about Robinson's view of the relationship between taste and morals?
5. Is stanza 4 criticism of Flammonde or of some of the people of 'Tilbury Town'?
6. What criticism is made?
7. In what way do the first two lines of stanza 5 provide an excellent example of compression?
8. What expression in stanza 6 indicates that the woman has a 'murky past'?
9. Would you take this stanza to contain a tribute to Flammonde?
10. Was it bad or good of him not to see 'the scarlet fringe' in the woman upon whom the town frowned?
11. What do you think the last two lines of this stanza mean?
12. In stanza 9, having enumerated some more of Flammonde's qualities, Robinson asks the questions, 'What small satanic sort

of kink / Was in his brain? What broken line / Withheld him from the destinies / That came so near to being his?' Would you say that Robinson has, by this point, told us enough about Flammonde to justify the assertion that he possesses a 'small satanic kink'? Or do you think that the question is his way of now informing us that Flammonde did, indeed, possess such a kink?

13. What kind of destinies might have been Flammonde's?

14. What, in stanza 11, does Robinson mean by complaining that not all Flammonde's good actions can quite make up for 'what was his, and his alone'?

15. What does Robinson mean when he says we all have a 'darkening hill to climb'? Is this true?

16. Do you find this a pessimistic or an optimistic poem?

17. State the paradox finally posed by the existence of Flammonde as Robinson saw it.

Thou still unravish'd bride of quietness,
   Thou foster-child of silence and slow time,
Sylvan historian, who canst thus express
   A flowery tale more sweetly than our rhyme:
What leaf-fring'd legend haunts about thy shape   5
   Of deities or mortals, or of both,
      In Tempe or the dales of Arcady?
   What men or gods are these? What maidens loth?
What mad pursuit? What struggle to escape?
      What pipes and timbrels? What wild ecstasy?   10

Heard melodies are sweet, but those unheard
   Are sweeter; therefore, ye soft pipes, play on;
Not to the sensual ear, but, more endear'd,
   Pipe to the spirit ditties of no tone:
Fair youth, beneath the trees, thou canst not leave   15
   Thy song, nor ever can those trees be bare;
      Bold Lover, never, never canst thou kiss,
Though winning near the goal—yet, do not grieve;
   She cannot fade, though thou hast not thy bliss,
      For ever wilt thou love, and she be fair!   20

Ah, happy, happy boughs! that cannot shed
   Your leaves, nor ever bid the Spring adieu;
And, happy melodist, unwearied,
   For ever piping songs for ever new;
More happy love! more happy, happy love!   25
   For ever warm and still to be enjoy'd,
      For ever panting, and for ever young;
All breathing human passion far above,
   That leaves a heart high-sorrowful and cloy'd,
      A burning forehead, and a parching tongue.   30

Who are these coming to the sacrifice?
   To what green altar, O mysterious priest,
Lead'st thou that heifer lowing at the skies,
   And all her silken flanks with garlands drest?

What little town by river or sea shore,   35
    Or mountain-built with peaceful citadel,
        Is emptied of this folk, this pious morn?
And, little town, thy streets for evermore
    Will silent be; and not a soul to tell
        Why thou art desolate, can e'er return.   40

O Attic shape! Fair attitude! with brede
    Of marble men and maidens overwrought,
With forest branches and the trodden weed;
    Thou, silent form, dost tease us out of thought
As doth eternity: Cold Pastoral!   45
    When old age shall this generation waste,
        Thou shalt remain, in midst of other woe
Than ours, a friend to man, to whom thou say'st,
    'Beauty is truth, truth beauty,'—that is all
        Ye know on earth, and all ye need to know.   50

Keats's odes, and perhaps especially this one, are judged by some critics to be the height of his achievement. Others, while admitting Keats's poetic genius, object to their romantic lushness. One critic has gone so far as to call all the odes, with the exception of the simplest one, *To Autumn*, 'higher spoof'. He meant that Keats was, basically, only imitating being a poet; that ultimately these poems were rhetorical. After you have read and discussed this poem in detail, and answered the questions below, give your view of this dictum. Is it absolutely fair? Is there an element of truth in it? Does it make any difference that Keats died at the age of twenty-five (twenty-one months after he wrote this ode), before he had had a chance to develop his full powers? But these are general questions, to be discussed after considering the poem in detail.

In *Ode to a Nightingale* Keats had contrasted the beauties of the natural world with the 'weariness, the fever, and the fret' of human existence; in this poem he contrasts its impermanence with the unchanging nature of the figures on an imaginary Greek vase. We know that he had no particular vase in mind, but that he combined features of various illustrations he had seen, both of vases and of French paintings, into an ideal urn.

Tempe (line 7)   a vale in Thessaly that frequently figures in mythology

Arcady (line 7)   refers to an even more famous Greek district, Arcadia

breathing (line 28)   living

1. Why does Keats state that the scene represented on the urn can express 'A flowery tale more sweetly than our rhyme'? To whom does 'our' refer? Why is not the urn also 'ours'?

2. What does 'Heard melodies are sweet, but those unheard / Are sweeter' mean? Is this true, or a typical piece of romantic exaggeration, calculated to build up a powerful but not necessarily meaningful effect?

3. In lines 19–20, why cannot 'She' fade? Why has the youth not had his 'bliss'? Does the poet imply that it is better to love 'For ever', and never have bliss?

4. Is 'O Attic shape! Fair attitude' musically clumsy, as has frequently been alleged, or is it, in the words of one critic, 'a deliberate use of sound in an almost Elizabethan way, in which Shakespeare would have delighted'?

5. Why, in line 45, is the Pastoral described as 'Cold'?

6. The final two lines of the poem express the message of the urn to those who behold it. Relate this message to the rest of the poem, put it into your own words, and say whether you consider it to be a valid one.

7. What archaisms—that is, expressions that were out of date even in Keats's time—can you discover in this poem? Do you think they heighten or lessen the effect Keats is trying to produce?

That's my last Duchess painted on the wall,
Looking as if she were alive. I call
That piece a wonder, now: Frà Pandolf's hands
Worked busily a day, and there she stands.
Will't please you sit and look at her? I said   5
'Frà Pandolf' by design, for never read
Strangers like you that pictured countenance,
The depth and passion of its earnest glance,
But to myself they turned (since none puts by
The curtain I have drawn for you, but I)   10
And seemed as they would ask me, if they durst,
How such a glance came there; so, not the first
Are you to turn and ask thus. Sir, 'twas not
Her husband's presence only, called that spot
Of joy into the Duchess' cheek: perhaps   15
Frà Pandolf chanced to say 'Her mantle laps
'Over my lady's wrist too much,' or 'Paint
'Must never hope to reproduce the faint
'Half-flush that dies along her throat:' such stuff
Was courtesy, she thought, and cause enough   20
For calling up that spot of joy. She had
A heart—how shall I say?—too soon made glad,
Too easily impressed; she liked whate'er
She looked on, and her looks went everywhere.
Sir, 'twas all one! My favour at her breast,   25
The dropping of the daylight in the West,
The bough of cherries some officious fool
Broke in the orchard for her, the white mule
She rode with round the terrace—all and each
Would draw from her alike the approving speech,   30
Or blush, at least. She thanked men,—good! but thanked
Somehow—I know not how—as if she ranked
My gift of a nine-hundred-years-old name
With anybody's gift. Who'd stoop to blame
This sort of trifling? Even had you skill   35
In speech—(which I have not)—to make your will
Quite clear to such an one, and say, 'Just this

'Or that in you disgusts me; here you miss,
'Or there exceed the mark'—and if she let
Herself be lessoned so, nor plainly set   40
Her wits to yours, forsooth, and made excuse,
—E'en then would be some stooping; and I choose
Never to stoop. Oh sir, she smiled, no doubt,
When'er I passed her; but who passed without
Much the same smile? This grew; I gave commands;   45
Then all smiles stopped together. There she stands
As if alive. Will't please you rise? We'll meet
The company below, then. I repeat,
The Count your master's known munificence
Is ample warrant that no just pretence   50
Of mine for dowry will be disallowed;
Though his fair daughter's self, as I avowed
At starting, is my object. Nay, we'll go
Together down, sir. Notice Neptune, though,
Taming a sea-horse, thought a rarity,   55
Which Claus of Innsbruck cast in bronze for me!

1. Who speaks this monologue and to whom?
2. For what purpose has the listener come?
3. Quote the line or lines which tell us that Frà Pandolf had painted a lifelike portrait?
4. Browning has often been accused of obscurity. Have a shot of paraphrasing lines 5 to 12.
5. Quote the line which tells us that the Duke sets store by his ancient lineage.
6. In what words does the speaker indicate, without saying as much, that he had had the Duchess murdered?
7. What alleged fault in her character caused him to do this?
8. Why did he not warn her before having her murdered?
9. Do you find any faults in the character of the Duchess?
10. We are not told why the speaker tells the listener of the fate of the Duchess. Why do you think he did so? In other words, what is the motive behind the monologue?
11. Consider carefully the words 'Nay, we'll go / Together down sir'. in lines 53-4. We think these casual words have significance: what is it? Begin by constructing an imaginary remark on the part of the listener to which 'Nay' is a reply.

12. Claus of Innsbruck is an imaginary sculptor. What work of his does the speaker name, and what is the effect of the mention of it?

13. Which of the following epithets can justly be applied to the character of the speaker? aesthetically philistine; amoral, arriviste; avaricious; chivalrous; cold; masochistic; munificent; musical; nouveau riche; philanthropic; proud; rumbustious; salacious; smooth; sophisticated.

14. What poetic advantage does Browning secure by the 'dramatic' method of revealing the speaker's character—i.e. the method of self-revelation?

15. Recount the whole episode as briefly as possible in the words of the listener, writing a despatch to a friend, beginning with the words 'When I called on . . .'

16. How much of Browning's own nature is revealed by this poem?

17. Wardour Street in Soho used to be known for its shops selling sham antiques. Browning's detractors have accused him of using what is called 'Wardour Street English'. Here he is putting nineteenth-century English into the mouth of an imaginary early Renaissance Italian nobleman. Does he perpetrate any examples of Wardour Street English?

18. Having read the poem in the light of these questions, read it aloud in the most expressive way you can.

19. Some of Browning's dramatic monologues have been called diffuse and verbose? Could this be said of *My Last Duchess*?

20. Do you consider the poem great? good? trivial? bad? Does it induce in you a desire to read more of Browning or find out more about him and his poetry? If so, read the penetrating biographical study by Betty Miller,* who gives cogent reasons for Browning's preference for obscurity and indirectness in poetry.

21. Write a short dramatic monologue of your own about a hypothetical character in any period of history. Rhymed couplets are not necessary: you may prefer to write blank verse.

* *Robert Browning: a Portrait* (John Murray, London 1952).

34. HENRY VAUGHAN: *Death. A Dialogue*

Soule.

'Tis a sad Land, that in one day
Hath dull'd thee thus, when death shall freeze
Thy bloud to Ice, and thou must stay
Tenant for Yeares, and Centuries,
How wilt thou brook't?—   5

Body.

I cannot tell,—
But if all sence wings not with thee,
And something still be left the dead,
I'le wish my Curtaines off to free
Me from so darke, and sad a bed;   10

A neast of nights, a gloomie sphere,
Where shadowes thicken, and the Cloud
Sits on the Suns brow all the yeare,
And nothing moves without a shrowd;

Soule.

'Tis so: But as thou sawest that night   15
Wee travell'd in, our first attempts
Were dull, and blind, but Custome straight
Our feares, and falls brought to contempt,

Then, when the gastly *twelve* was past
We breath'd still for a blushing *East*,   20
And bad the lazie Sunne make hast,
And on sure hopes, though long, did feast;

But when we saw the Clouds to crack
And in those Cranies light appear'd,
We thought the day then was not slack,   25
And pleas'd our selves with what wee feared;

Just so it is in death. But thou
Shalt in thy mothers bosome sleepe
Whilst I each minute grone to know
How neere Redemption creepes.   30

Then shall wee meet to mix again, and met,
'Tis last good-night, our Sunne shall never set.

Job: Chap. 10, ver. 21, 22.
Before I goe whence I shall not returne, even to the land of darknesse,
and the shadow of death;
A Land of darknesse, as darkenesse it selfe, and of the shadow of
death, without any order, and where the light is as darknesse.

Henry Vaughan, who called himself the silurist (from the seat of
his family in South Wales: 'Swan of Usk', *Olor Iscanus*), was a
Breconshire doctor who lived from 1622 until 1695. All but his
earliest and least good poems are on sacred subjects. He himself
acknowledged his debt to George Herbert. Vaughan, like Herbert,
is deeply and sincerely pious—but he is more mystical and medi-
tative. *Death* is a characteristic poem. The dialogue between the
soul and the body was a common form in the seventeenth century,
and was most notably used by Andrew Marvell.

This poem begins with the soul asking the body how it will
endure waiting, 'for Yeares, and Centuries', for its resurrection.
As distinct from Marvell's soul-body dialogues, the two entities
are not in disagreement. The body tells the soul that it does not
know how it will perform this feat of endurance; but it says that
if consciousness does not all fly away with the soul at the time
of death, then it hopes at least not to be left to rest in the dark,
sad earth. The soul, in its reply, agrees that the earth (i.e. the
consciousless condition of death, in which the personality is
totally obliterated) is indeed dark; it reminds the body of an
earlier journey through the night, in which all at first appeared
black, but in what at length all 'feares' and 'falls' were confounded,
so that when midnight passed, they awaited the dawn, which did
finally arrive.

The soul now draws a final comparison, between this night and
the death the long oblivion of which the body so fears. The
'mothers bosome' is the earth, and the soul states that the body
will have sound sleep in the earth, whereas it, in its consciousness,
will suffer every moment in awaiting the time of redemption, of
the resurrection when at last it and the body shall be united for
ever.

1. Is the poet on the side of the body or the soul, or neither? Would you call this an optimistic poem or a pessimistic poem?

2. The nature of the 'night' through which the earlier journey was taken is not made explicit. Is it the night of ignorance? Or of lack of faith? Or simply of suffering? Or pre-birth?

3. This poem is written within a framework of orthodox Christian belief. Few readers in its time would have questioned any of these beliefs; and there is nothing doctrinal in it that could then have offended theologically. Nowadays this framework of belief is no longer universal. Must we necessarily fail to appreciate the poem if we cannot enter into the beliefs upon which it depends?

4. Or is there another way of looking at it, by which we can take as the poem's subject-matter the not specifically Christian emotion of fear of death and of the subsequent allaying of that fear? If death be read as 'fear of death', then the poem can be read in this way, so that it does not make any speculations at all about actual death. But is this to wilfully misread and distort it?

5. Is the poem effective because of the writer's transparent sincerity and the ecstasy with which he writes, or because of his technical skill—or both?

35. WILLIAM WORDSWORTH: *A slumber did my spirit seal*

A slumber did my spirit seal;
  I had no human fears:
She seemed a thing that could not feel
  The touch of earthly years.

No motion has she now, no force;   5
  She neither hears nor sees;
Rolled round in earth's diurnal course,
  With rocks, and stones, and trees.

A. E. HOUSMAN: *The night is freezing fast*

The night is freezing fast,
  To-morrow comes December;
    And winterfalls of old
Are with me from the past;
  And chiefly I remember   5
    How Dick would hate the cold.

Fall, winter, fall; for he,
  Prompt hand and headpiece clever,
    Has woven a winter robe,
And made of earth and sea   10
  His overcoat for ever,
    And wears the turning globe.

1. What does 'diurnal' mean?
2. What does Housman mean by 'winterfalls'?
3. What reason does Wordsworth give for his spirit being sealed
by slumber, and his lack of human fears?
4. How does Housman say that Dick managed to overcome his
hatred of the cold? Was this clever of Dick? Can you detect any
form of irony in this poem?
5. If the word 'brain' had fitted the metre, would it have been as
effective a word as 'headpiece'?

6. Do you think Housman had Wordsworth's poem in mind when he wrote *The night is freezing fast?* Can he justly be accused of plagiarism?

7. What idea do these two poems have in common. Quote the relevant lines in each poem to illustrate your answer.

8. In what ways do the poet's treatment of this idea differ?

9. Does the philosophy behind Wordsworth's poem strike you as being optimistic or pessimistic—or neither? How would you describe it?

10. If the first poem may be summed up as tragic, what word would you use to sum up the second?

11. Is there anything in *The night is freezing fast* to justify the once common practice among readers of coupling Housman with Hardy (see pp. 62, 97)?

12. Which of the two poems do you prefer, and why?

36. ALFRED, LORD TENNYSON: *Tithonus*

The woods decay, the woods decay and fall,
The vapours weep their burthen to the ground,
Man comes and tills the field and lies beneath,
And after many a summer dies the swan.
Me only cruel immortality   5
Consumes: I wither slowly in thine arms,
Here at the quiet limit of the world,
A white-hair'd shadow roaming like a dream
The ever silent spaces of the East,
Far-folded mists, and gleaming halls of morn.   10

Alas! for this grey shadow, once a man—
So glorious in his beauty and thy choice,
Who madest him thy chosen, that he seem'd
To his great heart none other than a God!
I ask'd thee, 'Give me immortality.'   15
Then didst thou grant mine asking with a smile,
Like wealthy men who care not how they give.
But thy strong Hours indignant work'd their wills,
And beat me down and marr'd and wasted me,
And tho' they could not end me, left me maim'd   20
To dwell in presence of immortal youth,
Immortal age beside immortal youth,
And all I was, in ashes. Can thy love,
Thy beauty, make amends, tho' even now,
Close over us, the silver star, thy guide,   25
Shines in those tremulous eyes that fill with tears
To hear me? Let me go: take back thy gift:
Why should a man desire in any way
To vary from the kindly race of men,
Or pass beyond the goal of ordinance   30
Where all should pause, as is most meet for all?

A soft air fans the cloud apart; there comes
A glimpse of that dark world where I was born.
Once more the old mysterious glimmer steals
From thy pure brows, and from thy shoulders pure,   35

And bosom beating with a heart renew'd.
Thy cheek begins to redden thro' the gloom,
Thy sweet eyes brighten slowly close to mine,
Ere yet they blind the stars, and the wild team
Which love thee, yearning for thy yoke, arise,   40
And shake the darkness from their loosen'd manes,
And beat the twilight into flakes of fire.

   Lo! ever thus thou growest beautiful
In silence, then before thine answer given
Departest, and thy tears are on my cheek.   45

   Why wilt thou ever scare me with thy tears,
And make me tremble lest a saying learnt,
In days far-off, on that dark earth, be true?
'The Gods themselves cannot recall their gifts.'
Ay me! ay me! with what another heart   50
In days far-off, and with what other eyes
I used to watch—if I be he that watch'd—
The lucid outline forming round thee; saw
The dim curls kindly into sunny rings;
Changed with thy mystic change, and felt my blood   55
Glow with the glow, that slowly crimson'd all
Thy presence and thy portals, while I lay,
Mouth, forehead, eyelids, growing dewy-warm
With kisses balmier than half-opening buds
Of April, and could hear the lips that kiss'd   60
Whispering I knew not what of wild and sweet,
Like that strange song I heard Apollo sing,
While Ilion like a mist rose into towers.

   Yet hold me not for ever in thine East:
How can my nature longer mix with thine?   65
Coldly thy rosy shadows bathe me, cold
Are all thy lights, and cold my wrinkled feet
Upon thy glimmering thresholds, when the steam
Floats up from those dim fields about the homes
Of happy men that have the power to die,   70
And grassy barrows of the happier dead.
Release me, and restore me to the ground;
Thou seest all things, thou wilt see my grave:

Thou wilt renew thy beauty morn by morn;
I earth in earth forget these empty courts,   75
And thee returning on thy silver wheels.

Tithonus, the son of Laomedon and brother of Priam, King of
Troy, was loved by Eos, goddess of dawn (Aurora in Roman
mythology), who obtained from Zeus the gift of immortality for
him, but forgot to obtain also the gift of eternal youth.

1. In the first ten lines there is a summary of the whole purport
of the poem in two words. What are they?
2. In the first few lines there are three references to death. Men-
tion them.
3. What made Tithonus feel like a god when young?
4. Quote the simile or comparison you find most striking.
5. What indication is there that Aurora feels pity for her lover?
6. What is meant by the phrase 'the goal of ordinance' (line 30)?
7. What is 'the wild team' (line 39)?
8. What reference is there to the mythological belief that Troy
was built to the sound of divine music?
9. Tithonus is pleading with Aurora to have his immortality
ended. Nevertheless, he half suspects that she has not this power.
How do we know this?
10. Swift's prose satire, *Gulliver's Travels*, Part III, contains a
striking passage in which one of the inhabitants of Luggnagg
describes the situation of the Struldbrugs or immortals. Compare
this with Tennyson's version.

He said they commonly acted like mortals, till about thirty years
old, after which by degrees they grew melancholy and dejected,
increasing in both till they came to fourscore. . . . When they came
to fourscore years, which is reckoned the extremity of living in this
country, they had not only all the follies and infirmities of other old
men, but many more which arose from the dreadful prospect of
never dying. They were not only opinionative, peevish, covetous,
morose, vain, talkative, but uncapable of friendship and dead to all
natural affection, which never descended below their grandchildren.
Envy and impotent desires are their prevailing passions. But those
objects against which their envy seems principally directed are the

vices of the younger sort, and the deaths of the old. By reflecting
on the former they find themselves cut off from all possibility of
pleasure: and whenever they see a funeral, they lament and repine
that others have gone to a harbour of rest to which they themselves
never can hope to arrive.

11. Line 9 contains no fewer than four long or open vowel
sounds. What effect was Tennyson aiming at?

12. Justify the unnatural grammatical inversion at the beginning
of line 5.

13. Quote two or three archaisms. Why does Tennyson use
them? Do you find them objectionable?

14. Tennyson has always been celebrated for his extreme power
of verbal suggestion—of underlining his sense by onomatopoeia
and vowel variation. What lines do you find most effective in
this way? Which, if any, do you find ineffective?

15. Has the poem a message for modern readers? If so, what?

16. Tennyson was attracted by many themes from classical
mythology. Read *Oenone* and *The Lotus Eaters* and say which
you find most satisfying—*Tithonus* or one or both of these two.

37. WILLIAM BLAKE: *Holy Thursday* I

'Twas on a Holy Thursday, their innocent faces clean,
The children walking two & two, in red & blue & green,
Grey-headed beadles walk'd before, with wands as white as snow,
Till into the high dome of Paul's they like Thames' waters flow.

O what a multitude they seem'd, these flowers of London town! 5
Seated in companies they sit with radiance all their own.
The hum of multitudes was there, but multitudes of lambs,
Thousands of little boys & girls raising their innocent hands.

Now like a mighty wind they raise to heaven the voice of song,
Or like harmonious thunderings the seats of heaven among. 10
Beneath them sit the aged men, wise guardians of the poor;
Then cherish pity, lest you drive an angel from your door.

Holy Thursday II

Is this a holy thing to see
In a rich and fruitful land,
Babes reduc'd to misery,
Fed with cold and usurous hand?

Is that trembling cry a song? 5
Can it be a song of joy?
And so many children poor?
It is a land of poverty!

And their sun does never shine,
And their fields are bleak & bare, 10
And their ways are fill'd with thorns:
It is eternal winter there.

For where-e'er the sun does shine,
And where-e'er the rain does fall,
Babe can never hunger there, 15
Nor poverty the mind appall.

123

1. Blake published these two parallel poems in his two collections, *Songs of Innocence* and *Songs of Experience*. Which comes from which?

2. In Version I line 4, what is the significance of the simile 'like Thames' waters'?

3. The beadles' staffs of office are called 'wands as white as snow'. Why?

4. In line 5 the children are described metaphorically as 'flowers'. To what line in stanza 1 does this look back?

5. If the keynote of Version I is 'pity'—pity for the children of the poor, who attended the newly-opened charity schools in London and were taken to an annual Ascension Day service in St Paul's—what would you say is the keynote, the pervading emotion of Version II? N.B. The word is not necessarily in the poem itself.

6. What lines in Version II indicate that Blake was familiar with the language of the Bible?

7. The versification of both versions is irregular, especially in rhythm. Is this a good or a bad thing in this instance?

8. How do you account for the fact that one poet wrote both these versions? Are they inconsistent?

9. Is either version to be regarded as propaganda? Is any purpose to be served by writing didactic poetry with a social content?

10. Which do you think the more moving of these two poems?

Tyr'd with all these for restfull death I cry
As to behold desert a begger borne,
And needie Nothing trim'd in jollitie,
And purest faith unhappily forsworne,
And gilded honor shamefully misplast,   5
And maiden vertue rudely strumpeted,
And right perfection wrongfully disgrac'd,
And strength by limping sway disabled,
And arte made tung-tide by authoritie,
And Folly (Doctor-like) controlling skill,   10
And simple-Truth miscalde Simplicitie,
And captive-good attending Captaine ill.
    Tyr'd with all these, from these would I be gone,
    Save that to dye, I leave my love alone.

There has been as much controversy about the origins and cir-
cumstances of publication of Shakespeare's sonnet-sequence as
about any group of poems. The sonnets appeared in 1609, and it
is likely that their author had nothing to do with their publication.
We have chosen one of the comparatively few non-personal son-
nets, one that seems to have been written in a mood of extreme
general depression.

This poet is clearly not only depressed, however, but also
cynical. 'Desert' has only the status of a beggar. Faith and
honour are betrayed. 'Needie nothing' is 'trim'd in jollitie', i.e.
clothed in finery. Virtue is taken advantage of, true simplicity
dismissed as mere rustic folly. (Note that 'disabled' is pro-
nounced with four syllables.)

1. What does 'these' in line 1 refer to?
2. Do you think that, if 'arte' can mean simply 'literature', the
line 'And arte made tung-tide by authoritie', means 'writers are
unable to speak the truth because they will be deprived of their
livelihood by the establishment?' Or does it simply refer to the
practice of censorship?

3. Is art still tongue-tied by authority today?

4. Ought this to be so, to a certain extent, or is the absolute freedom of writers and artists an essential liberty? If so why?

5. Do you agree with one commentator's remark on the phrase 'Doctor-like' in line 10: 'with the knowing air of a doctor, i.e. most experts are quacks'?

6. What attitude does the poet have to the person he loves if he does not wish to leave this person alone in such a world as he has here depicted?

7. Is this picture of the world true of today—or has the poem lost its point?

8. Have you ever felt in the mood of this poem, and if you have, would you consider writing a poem about it? Or do you think that this poet was wasting his time by giving vent to greatly exaggerated and negative feelings?

9. If you believe the poet is right in his attitude, and that the poem is an effective one, give examples, from today's world, of each of the charges he makes against humanity.

10. What elements in the poem, if any, offer a gleam of hope?

11. At what kind of period in history do you think this poem was written? Give reasons for your answer.

12. Would it help us in understanding the poem if we could be told any definite facts about the author and his situation at the time he wrote it?

    In flow'd at once a gay embroider'd race,   275
And titt'ring push'd the Pedants off the place:
Some would have spoken, but the voice was drown'd
By the French horn, or by the op'ning hound.
The first came forwards, with as easy mien,
As if he saw St. James's and the Queen.   280
When thus th' attendant Orator begun.
'Receive, great Empress! thy accomplish'd Son:
Thine from the birth, and sacred from the rod,
A dauntless infant! never scar'd with God.
The Sire saw, one by one, his Virtues wake: 285
The Mother begg'd the blessing of a Rake.
Thou gav'st that Ripeness, which so soon began,
And ceas'd so soon, he ne'er was Boy, nor Man.
Thro' School and College, thy kind cloud o'ercast,
Safe and unseen the young Æneas past: 290
Thence bursting glorious, all at once let down,
Stunn'd with his giddy Larum half the town.
Intrepid then, o'er seas and lands he flew:
Europe he saw, and Europe saw him too.
There all thy gifts and graces we display,   295
Thou, only thou, directing all our way!
To where the Seine, obsequious as she runs,
Pours at great Bourbon's feet her silken sons;
Or Tyber, now no longer Roman, rolls,
Vain of Italian Arts, Italian Souls: 300
To happy Convents, bosom'd deep in vines,
Where slumber Abbots, purple as their wines:
To Isles of fragrance, lilly-silver'd vales,
Diffusing languor in the panting gales:
To lands of singing, or of dancing slaves,   305
Love-whisp'ring woods, and lute-resounding waves.
But chief her shrine where naked Venus keeps,
And cupids ride the Lyon of the Deeps;
Where, eas'd of Fleets, the Adriatic main
Wafts the smooth Eunuch and enamour'd swain.   310

Led by my hand, he saunter'd Europe round,
And gather'd ev'ry Vice on Christian ground;
Saw ev'ry Court, heard ev'ry King declare
His royal Sense, of Op'ra's or the Fair;
The Stews and Palace equally explor'd,   315
Intrigu'd with glory, and with spirit whor'd;
Try'd all *hors-d' œuvres*, all *liqueurs* defin'd,
Judicious drank, and greatly-daring din'd;
Dropt the dull lumber of the Latin store,
Spoil'd his own language, and acquired no more;   320
All Classic learning lost on Classic ground;
And last turn'd *Air*, the Echo of a Sound!
See now, half-cur'd, and perfectly well-bred,
With nothing but a Solo in his head;
As much Estate, and Principle, and Wit,   325
As Jansen, Fleetwood, Cibber shall think fit;
Stol'n from a Duel, follow'd by a Nun,
And, if a Borough chuse him, not undone;
See, to my country happy I restore
This glorious Youth, and add one Venus more.   330

This extract from *The Dunciad* includes a description of the Grand Tour of Europe which was taken by rich and aristocratic young men in the eighteenth century. *The Dunciad* is a satire on now sometimes obscure habits, customs and people. Before we can ask questions on this passage, therefore, we must take up an unusually large amount of space with explanatory notes.

278 *op'ning* barking
279–80 *as . . . Queen* probably a satirical allusion to Frederick, Prince of Wales' well-known quarrel with his parents, and to his behaviour when in the Royal presence
281 *Orator* probably an enemy of Pope's called J. D. Breval, a don, poetaster, playwright, journalist, soldier and lover of a nun who left her convent for him (see line 327); he had called Pope 'in Form a Monkey, but for spite, a Toad'
282 *Empress* dullness, the subject of *The Dunciad*
286 The Mother hoped her son would become a rake

288 Dullness, Pope says in his own note to this line, annihilates both Infancy and Manhood

292 *Larum* alarm. This is a reference to the noisy rakes up-setting everyone's sleep

299–300 Things have deteriorated so much that the Tiber, no longer Roman, is proud of *Italian* arts and souls

303 *lilly-silver'd vales* vales abundant in tuberoses

307–8 Venice, whose coat of arms was a winged lion, was famous as 'the brothel of Europe', much visited of course by young men on their Grand Tours

315 *Stews* brothels

317 *hors-d'œuvres* the first literary use of this word in its present meaning

318 *greatly-daring din'd* foreign food, with its 'disguised ingredients', was reckoned to be 'highly inflammatory and un-wholesome'

326 *Jansen, Fleetwood, Cibber* 'Three very eminent persons, all Managers of *Plays*' (Pope). All three were notorious gamblers

328 *a Borough chuse him* M.P.'s were immune from arrest for debt

1. Pick out all the words and phrases in the first six lines that you consider make it apparent that this passage is wholly satiri-cal in intention.

2. Why does Pope call the race that 'push'd the Pedants off the place' 'gay' and 'embroider'd'?

3. Of what kind of people does the word 'titt'ring' suggest that this 'gay embroider'd race' consists?

4. Quote three or four separate lines exemplifying Pope's talent for antithesis.

5. In what lines does Pope satirize the current craze for Italian opera?

6. Find a reference to political elections.

7. What unnatural attitude is described in lines 281–286?

8. Why do you think Pope referred to his young Grand Tourist as Æneas (line 290)?

9. In what ways does the poetry of this passage differ from that of the Romantic Movement? What are its merits, and how high do you rate it?

10. Can you tell from this passage whether Pope himself had been on the Grand Tour?

11. What do you think is Pope's personal attitude to the Grand Tour as a means of further education?

12. From this account, do you yourself think it was a bad institution?

13. Quote the lines that indicate favourite occupations of the sprigs of the nobility. Which lines do you find most graphic?

I dreamed that, as I wandered by the way,
   Bare Winter suddenly was changed to Spring,
And gentle odours led my steps astray,
   Mixed with a sound of waters murmuring
Along a shelving bank of turf, which lay   5
   Under a copse, and hardly dared to fling
Its green arms round the bosom of the stream,
But kissed it and then fled, as thou mightest in dream.

There grew pied wind-flowers and violets,
   Daisies, those pearled Arcturi of the earth,   10
The constellated flower that never sets;
   Faint oxslips; tender bluebells, at whose birth
The sod scarce heaved; and that tall flower that wets—
   Like a child, half in tenderness and mirth—
Its mother's face with Heaven's collected tears,   15
When the low wind, its playmate's voice, it hears.

And in the warm hedge grew lush eglantine,
   Green cowbind and the moonlight-coloured may,
And cherry-blossoms, and white cups, whose wine
   Was the bright dew, yet drained not by the day;   20
And wild roses, and ivy serpentine,
   With its dark buds and leaves, wandering astray;
And flowers azure, black, and streaked with gold,
Fairer than any wakened eyes behold.

And nearer to the river's trembling edge   25
   There grew broad flag-flowers, purple pranked with white,
And starry river buds among the sedge,
   And floating water-lilies, broad and bright,
Which lit the oak that overhung the hedge
   With moonlight beams of their own watery light;   30
And bulrushes, and reeds of such deep green
As soothed the dazzled eye with sober sheen.

Methought that of these visionary flowers
   I made a nosegay, bound in such a way
That the same hues, which in their natural bowers   35
   Were mingled or opposed, the like array
Kept these imprisoned children of the Hours
   Within my hand,—and then, elate and gay,
I hastened to the spot whence I had come,
That I might there present it!—Oh! to whom?   40

1. This poem (written in 1820) is by a Romantic poet. What traces, if any, of eighteenth-century vocabulary or phrasing does it bear?

2. In line 26 the word 'pranked' occurs. What does it mean? Make your own definition, based on its use in this poem, and compare it with that of the dictionary.

3. What phrase does Shelley use to convey the notion of flowers as belonging only to a particular season?

4. What example of personification is contained in stanza 1? Do you think it is effective in adding to the description, or merely fanciful?

5. An impossible event is stated to have taken place. How does Shelley justify this record of it?

6. How did the flowers attract the narrator's interest in the first place?

7. Arcturus is a very white star. Does Shelley mention any other characteristic of the daisy that makes this an effective comparison?

8. What does the poet mean by 'its mother's face'?

9. You have answered question 5. In what line in stanza 3 does the narrator allude again to the reason for his strange experience? What new impossible elements are introduced?

10. How (lines 34–7) was the nosegay bound?

11. In lines 13–16 there is a metaphor of a child, a mother and a playmate. Explain this. Is it truthful? Is it striking and effective?

12. Why (line 33) are the flowers 'visionary'?

13. The poem is called *The Question*. There are two interpretations of the last line. One asserts that the question, 'Oh! to whom?' is one of despair. What state of mind would this imply? The other suggests that the poem was written in the midwinter

of 1819–20 and addressed to a particular woman, Sophia Stacey.
What then would the final question imply? Which interpretation
do you favour? Are there any circumstances in which both inter-
pretations could be right?

14. What echoes of Shakespearean flower-imagery are there in
this poem?

41. RUPERT BROOKE: *The Dead*

Blow out, you bugles, over the rich Dead!
There's none of these so lonely and poor of old,
But, dying, has made us rarer gifts than gold.
These laid the world away; poured out the red
Sweet wine of youth; gave up the years to be   5
Of work and joy, and that unhoped serene,
That men call age; and those who would have been,
Their sons, they gave, their immortality.

Blow, bugles, blow! They brought us, for our dearth,
Holiness, lacked so long, and Love, and Pain.   10
Honour has come back, as a king, to earth,
And paid his subjects with a royal wage;
And Nobleness walks in our ways again;
And we have come into our heritage.

1914

WILFRED OWEN: *Dulce et Decorum Est*

Bent double, like old beggars under sacks,
Knock-kneed, coughing like hags, we cursed through sludge,
Till on the haunting flares we turned our backs,
And towards our distant rest began to trudge.
Men marched asleep. Many had lost their boots,   5
But limped on, blood-shod. All went lame, all blind;
Drunk with fatigue; deaf even to the hoots
Of gas-shells dropping softly behind.

Gas! GAS! Quick, boys!—an ecstasy of fumbling,
Fitting the clumsy helmets just in time,   10
But someone still was yelling out and stumbling
And floundering like a man in fire or lime.—
Dim through the misty panes and thick green light,
As under a green sea, I saw him drowning.

In all my dreams before my helpless sight   15
He plunges at me, guttering, choking, drowning.

If in some smothering dreams, you too could pace
Behind the wagon that we flung him in,
And watch the white eyes writhing in his face,
His hanging face, like a devil's sick of sin;   20
If you could hear, at every jolt, the blood
Come gargling from the forth-corrupted lungs,
Bitter as the cud
Of vile, incurable sores on innocent tongues,—
My friend, you would not tell with such high zest   25
To children ardent for some desperate glory,
The old Lie: Dulce et decorum est
Pro patria mori.

1. Both of these poems are about dying for one's country in war. The first was written during the first few months of the 1914–18 war, the second during the last phase of the same war. Each represents very fairly the mood of the country and some of the men at the front during these two phases in the war. How do you account for the gap between them?

2. Which of the two would you say arises from the closer experience of war?

3. The first poem is an expression of idealism. Is there any idealism in the second?

4. Which words in *The Dead* speak of idealism?

5. The first section of *The Dead* lists the sacrifices made by the dead. Which line naming one of these sacrifices do you consider the most poignant?

6. The second section of *The Dead* mentions certain abstractions. Name these, and say whether you think their inclusion adds to, or subtracts from the effectiveness of the poem.

7. *The Dead* is a sonnet. Do you consider that, from a technical point of view, Brooke handles the form skilfully? If so why?

8. Locate the source of the quotation in the last two lines and the title of the second poem.

9. In line 2 we meet the pronoun 'we', and in line 17 we first

meet the pronoun 'you': what is the effect of these 'we's' and 'you's'?

10. Wordsworth said that a poet must have his eye on the object: does Owen maintain complete objectivity throughout the poem?

11. Point out three similes or comparisons beginning with 'like' or containing 'as', and say how effective you find them.

12. Since these poems were written, the cinema has been perfected and television has been invented. Films have been shown depicting scenes like the one described in *Dulce et Decorum Est*. Do you consider that a poem such as this has been outdated by the screen? What would be lost and what gained by transferring the scene to the screen?

13. Owen said that his poems were about the pity of war, and that the poetry is in the pity. Discuss his poem in the light of this saying. Does the poem express any emotion other than pity on the part of the poet?

14. Both Brooke and Owen died young, before the end of World War I. Which, in your opinion, would have had the greater future as a poet had he lived?

42. WILLIAM COWPER: *The Shrubbery*

Written in a Time of Affliction

Oh happy shades! to me unblest,
　　Friendly to peace, but not to me,
How ill the scene that offers rest,
　　And heart that cannot rest, agree!

This glassy stream, that spreading pine,　　　　5
　　Those alders quiv'ring to the breeze,
Might soothe a soul less hurt than mine,
　　And please, if any thing could please.

But fixt unalterable care
　　Foregoes not what she feels within,　　　　10
Shows the same sadness ev'ry where,
　　And slights the season and the scene.

For all that pleas'd in wood or lawn,
　　While peace possess'd these silent bow'rs,
Her animating smile withdrawn,　　　　15
　　Has lost its beauties and its pow'rs.

The saint or moralist should tread
　　This moss-grown alley, musing slow;
They seek, like me, the secret shade,
　　But not, like me, to nourish woe.　　　　20

Me fruitful scenes and prospects waste
　　Alike admonish not to roam;
These tell me of enjoyment past,
　　And those of sorrows yet to come.

1. This apparently simply and straightforward poem conceals much artistry. For instance, in stanza 1 Cowper repeats only two words (apart from the unimportant preposition 'to'). What are they, and how does their repetition affect the meaning of the poem?

2. The word-order is for the most part completely natural, i.e. that of simple prose. Point out the lines where there are poetic inversions. Do these mar or improve the effect?

3. In what way do the saint and the moralist differ from Cowper?

4. In eighteenth-century schools the composition of Latin verse was aided by the use of a standard textbook called *Gradus ad Parnassum* (*Steps to Parnassus*). It supplied lists of alternative epithets for use with frequently used nouns. Thus with the word for 'wind' would appear the Latin for 'keen', 'loud', 'gentle', etc., and any of these could be used more or less indiscriminately according as it fitted into the verse-pattern. This had a disastrous effect on the composition of minor verse-writers throughout the century. 'Sheep' were usually 'fleecy', the sun's beams were often 'radiant', a meadow was referred to as a 'grassy' or 'verdant' plain. These stock adjectives, or 'gradus epithets', as they have been termed, were the bane of mediocre verse and even got into the lines of some otherwise respectable poets—the young Pope, Johnson, Gray, for instance. Can Cowper be charged with using gradus epithets in this poem?

5. The over-use of epithets, good and bad, is often the weakness of descriptive poetry. To what nouns does Cowper apply no adjectives where he might have done, had the rhythm permitted? Does this make the lines stronger or weaker?

6. To which noun does Cowper apply two epithets, instead of his usual one? What is the effect of this? Is it tautological?

7. By what comparison does Cowper show his dread of the future? '*Written in a time of affliction*': after reading this subtitle, would you expect the rhythm of the poem to be regular or irregular: Which in fact is it? Is there enough variety in pace? If so, how does Cowper achieve it?

8. The excessive use of personification is another weakness of some eighteenth-century poetry. Point out two abstract nouns in this poem which Cowper has personified. Does it matter here? Why are they made feminine rather than masculine? What is the antecedent of the possessive adjective 'its' in line 16?

9. Is the basic emotion behind the poem one of self-pity? This is not something we usually admire in our friends. Can self-pity

in poetry be justified? If so, how? You should look up Cowper's personal history in a literary reference book.

10. Does this poem evoke our sympathy for the writer?

11. Does the poem transcend the limitations of poetic practice towards the end of the eighteenth century, or is Cowper imprisoned by them? Do they impose restrictions on his sincerity?

12. Would it be possible to write a poem such as this without having experienced personal suffering? Does it matter that we are not told the nature and cause of the 'affliction'?

From here through tunnelled gloom the track
Forks into two; and one of these
Wheels onward into darkening hills,
And one toward distant seas.

How still it is; the signal light   5
At set of sun shines palely green;
A thrush sings; other sound there's none,
Nor traveller to be seen—

Where late there was a throng. And now,
In peace awhile, I sit alone;   10
Though soon, at the appointed hour,
I shall myself be gone.

But not their way: the bow-legged groom,
The parson in black, the widow and son,
The sailor with his cage, the gaunt   15
Gamekeeper with his gun,

That fair one, too, discreetly veiled—
All, who so mutely came, and went,
Will reach those far nocturnal hills,
Or shores, ere night is spent.   20

I nothing know why thus we met—
Their thoughts, their longings, hopes, their fate:
And what shall I remember, except—
The evening growing late—

That here through tunnelled gloom the track   25
Forks into two; of these
One into darkening hills leads on,
And one toward distant seas?

This is a problem poem, whose meaning is grammatically clear, but whose significance is obscure. It consists of a series of plain statements by an 'I' (whom we call the speaker), all simple in themselves but adding up to a puzzle of some depth and intricacy. Write an appreciation and an explanation of the poem with the help of some or all of the following questions. We do not claim to be certain as to the answers to some of them, or even whether they have answers. We do not want to suggest that it should be turned into a prose story: it is a poem and stands or falls as such. But to understand its significance, its prose meaning must be grasped. You are as likely to arrive at a valid explanation as we.

1. The track forks into two. Which way have the travellers gone and which way is the speaker going at 'the appointed hour'?
2. What does the speaker mean by 'the appointed hour'?
3. Is there any symbolic significance in the 'hills', 'the seas', the signal light at green, the thrush's song, the time of day?
4. Is the group named in stanzas 4 and 5 a chance assembly, or is there some significance in the choice of these particular men and women? For what purpose have the group assembled? Why 'bow-legged', 'gaunt'? Why does the sailor have a cage? Why did they come and go 'mutely'?
5. Who is the speaker? What is the significance of the railway track and the junction?
6. Do these questions raise unnecessary difficulties? Do you find the poem puzzling? simple? haunting? memorable? impressive? unimpressive? a success or a failure? Do you think de la Mere himself knew what his poem was about?

44. DANTE GABRIEL ROSSETTI: *The Woodspurge*

The wind flapped loose, the wind was still,
Shaken out dead from tree and hill
I had walked on at the wind's will,—
I sat now, for the wind was still.

Between my knees my forehead was,—   5
My lips, drawn in, said not Alas!
My hair was over in the grass,
My naked ears heard the day pass.

My eyes, wide open, had the run
Of some ten weeds to fix upon;   10
Among those few, out of the sun,
The woodspurge flowered, three cups in one.

From perfect grief there need not be
Wisdom or even memory:
One thing then learnt remains to me,—   15
The woodspurge has a cup of three.

This poem was first published in Rossetti's 1870 volume, *Poems*.
The English son of Italian immigrant parents, Rossetti (1828–
1882) was a painter as well as a poet. He never really recovered
from the blow of his unstable and sick wife's suicide; later in life
he suffered from a serious mental breakdown, and became
addicted to a sedative drug, chloral, which he used to take in
whisky. His sister, Christina Rossetti, was also a distinguished
poet. Most of the poems for which Rossetti was praised in his
lifetime, such as *The Blessed Damozel*, are 'soft and styleless'; but
there was another side to his work, at once harder and more
lyrical, which is apparent in such poems as the early narrative,
A Last Confession, the late and unfinished *The Orchard Pit*, and
The Woodspurge.

1. What kind of day is the poet describing? Use as far as possible the words of the poem in your answer.

2. What does Rossetti mean when he says that the wind was 'Shaken out dead from tree and hill'?

3. What can we say, from the poem, about the nature of the landscape?

4. Describe how the poet walked. Why did he sit down?

5. What kind of mood was he in? Give precise reasons for your answer.

6. Does the fact that Rossetti did not say 'Alas!' mean that he was not in despair?

7. What justification do you think there is for the use of the phrase 'naked ears'?

8. Describe a woodspurge in the words of the poem.

9. What do you think Rossetti means by 'perfect grief'?

10. It might be said that to learn that the woodspurge 'has a cup of three' is a trivial and unimportant piece of knowledge, in any case perfectly obvious. What does Rossetti mean, and why does he present his experience as meaningful?

11. Can you think of an experience of your own that in any way parallels this one of Rossetti's? Try to record it in verse or prose.

Ther was also a Nonne, a PRIORESSE,
That of hir smylyng was ful symple and coy;
Hire gretteste ooth was but by Seinte Loy;   120
And she was cleped madame Eglentyne.
Ful weel she soong the service dyvyne,
Entuned in hir nose ful semely,
And Frenssh she spak ful faire and fetishly,
After the scole of Stratford atte Bowe,   125
For Frenssh of Parys was to hire unknowe.
At mete wel ytaught was she with alle:
She leet no morsel from hir lippes falle,
Ne wette hir fyngres in hir sauce depe;
Wel koude she carie a morsel and wel kepe   130
That no drope ne fille upon hire brest.
In curteisie was set ful muchel hir lest.
Hir over-lippe wyped she so clene
That in hir coppe ther was no ferthyng sene
Of grece, whan she dronken hadde hir draughte.   135
Ful semely after hir mete she raughte.
And sikerly she was of greet desport,
And ful plesaunt, and amyable of port,
And peyned hire to countrefete cheere
Of court, and to been estatlich of manere,   140
And to ben holden digne of reverence.
But, for to speken of hire conscience,
She was so charitable and so pitous
She wolde wepe, if that she saugh a mous
Kaught in a trappe, if it were deed or bledde.   145
Of smale houndes hadde she that she fede
With rosted flessh, or milk and wastel-breed.
But soore wepte she if oon of hem were deed,
Or if men smoot it with a yerde smerte;
And al was conscience and tendre herte.   150
Ful semyly hir wympul pynched was;
Hir nose tretys, hir eyen greye as glas,
Hir mouth ful smal, and therto softe and reed;

But sikerly she hadde a fair forheed;
It was almoost a spanne brood, I trowe;   155
For, hardily, she was nat undergrowe.
Ful fetys was hir cloke, as I was war.
Of smal coral aboute hire arm she bar
A peire of bedes, gauded al with grene,
And theron heng a brooch of gold ful sheene,   160
On which ther was first write a crowned A,
And after *Amor vincet omnia*.

Here is Chaucer's portrait of the Prioress, the head of a convent.
We are told of her appearance, her temperament and her sen-
sibility. The first thing we are told is that she smiled in a coy
and simple manner: she was evidently anxious to please and to
make a favourable impression. She did not swear (an odd thing
to note in a nun) more strongly than by the name of St Eligius,
patron saint of goldsmiths, farriers, etc. She intoned the divine
service in the somewhat nasal style favoured in the Middle Ages,
and spoke French, not as it is spoken in Paris, but in the Anglo-
Norman pronunciation adopted by the Benedictine convent of
St Leonard's at Bow in East London. This does not imply a
sneer at her French pronunciation, but perhaps Chaucer is being
gently ironic. Next we are given an account of her table-manners:
she reached in a 'semely' way for her food, of which none was
allowed to drop from her lips on to her breast; she saw to it that
no drop of fat was allowed to fall into her glass.

1. What conclusions do you draw from this account as to table-
manners generally in the later fourteenth century?
2. Once more we are told that the Prioress was 'of great desport',
amiable and pleasant in demeanour. Is it reasonable to regard
the Prioress, in the light of this account and what follows, as
worldly? To what extent ought a nun to be conscious of social
niceties?
3. She consciously adopted the style and manner of the Court?
Can she be regarded as, in the modern sense, a snob?
4. In line 142 we are introduced to her 'conscience'—what we
might call her sensibility—which was extremely alert to the
sufferings of animals and the cruelties of men towards small

creatures. She was called 'charitable' and 'pitous' in her feeling towards mice caught in traps. What is Chaucer's attitude here? Is he laughing at the Prioress? Is he praising her? Is he poking gentle fun at the attitude of women towards such matters, which a mere man might regard as of small consequence? Does he imply that mice were to her more important than human beings? Can her attitude to her own little dogs be regarded as affected or sentimental? Is Chaucer here simply *describing* or commenting?

5. Is Chaucer being simply objective, or approving, or censorious, in his account of her appearance—the neatly pleated wimple (head-covering), the fashionable glass-grey eyes, the well-formed nose, the narrow attractive mouth, the broad forehead?

6. In the description of the Prioress's dress Chaucer notes the neatness and worldliness of the Prioress. Undoubtedly jewellery was regarded, at this time, as, if not actually sinful, decidedly worldly for a woman professing a religious vocation. He takes pains to notice her coral beads and her rosary, in which a 'piere' (i.e. necklace, not simply two) of beads contained a gold brooch inscribed with the pagan Virgilian motto 'Love conquers all', surmounted with the letter 'A', probably meaning 'Amor'. Elsewhere in the *Prologue* it is clear that Chaucer held definite views about the nature of religious service: the Parson arouses him to something like anger when he contemplates the wicked clergy of his time. He is scathing about friars who exploit the poor and monks who merely love hunting, about ecclesiastical functionaries such as the Summoner who use their position for purposes of extortion. Chaucer was, first, a man. But he was also a poet, dedicated to looking objectively at the human scene and the human comedy. Do you think he lets the Prioress off lightly? His Prioress is obviously a very attractive woman and perhaps not a very religious one. Is his attitude one of ironical censure or of whole-hearted approval? Or is he wholly detached, refusing to take sides in any discussion of how far a Prioress ought to concern herself with matters of courtly behaviour and interest in clothes and jewellery? Or does he write simply as a commentator in an age of Catholicism, in which the job of Prioress is just a job like any other, whether in or out of established religion? Do you detect any note of censure in his account of her?

7. It is clear that Chaucer talked with many of his pilgrims. What evidence is there that he actually talked with the Prioress? Or did he simply observe her at table, as a fellow-pilgrim?

8. This passage, like the rest of the *Prologue,* is written in rhymed pentameters. Is it poetry? Is there anything in it in its present form that would have been lost if it had been written in prose?

9. The Prioress's tale is given in *The Canterbury Tales.* What sort of story do you think she would have told (assuming you have not already read it)? Look it up and read it (it is quite short and easy to follow). Is it what you would have expected from her?

Ere on my bed my limbs I lay,
It hath not been my use to pray
With moving lips or bended knees;
But silently, by slow degrees,
My spirit I to Love compose,   5
In humble trust mine eye-lids close,
With reverential resignation,
No wish conceived, no thought exprest,
Only a sense of supplication;
A sense o'er all my soul imprest   10
That I am weak, yet not unblest,
Since in me, round me, every where
Eternal strength and wisdom are.

But yester-night I prayed aloud
In anguish and in agony,   15
Up-starting from the fiendish crowd
Of shapes and thoughts that tortured me:
A lurid light, a trampling throng,
Sense of intolerable wrong,
And whom I scorned, those only strong!   20
Thirst of revenge, the powerless will
Still baffled, and yet burning still!
Desire with loathing strangely mixed
On wild or hateful objects fixed.
Fantastic passions! maddening brawl!   25
And shame and terror over all!
Deeds to be hid which were not hid,
Which all confused I could not know,
Whether I suffered, or I did:
For all seemed guilt, remorse or woe,   30
My own or others still the same
Life-stifling fear, soul-stifling shame.

So two nights passed: the night's dismay
Saddened and stunned the coming day.

Sleep, the wide blessing, seemed to me 35
Distemper's worst calamity.
The third night, when my own loud scream
Had waked me from the fiendish dream,
O'ercome with sufferings strange and wild,
I wept as I had been a child; 40
And having thus by tears subdued
My anguish to a milder mood,
Such punishments, I said, were due
To natures deepliest stained with sin,—
For aye entempesting anew 45
The unfathomable hell within
The horror of their deeds to view,
To know and loathe, yet wish and do!
Such griefs with such men well agree,
But wherefore, wherefore fall on me? 50
To be beloved is all I need,
And whom I love, I love indeed.

From a letter to Robert Southey

'I do not know how I came to scribble down these verses to you
—my heart was aching, my head all confused—but they are,
doggrels as they may be, a true portrait of my nights.—What to
do, I am at a loss:—for it is hard thus to be withered, having the
faculties & attainments, which I have.'

From a letter to Thomas Poole

'God forbid that my worst Enemy should ever have the Nights
& the Sleeps that I have had, night after night—surprised by Sleep,
while I struggled to remain awake, starting up to bless my own
loud Screams that had awakened me—yea, dear friend! till my
repeated Night-yells had made me a Nuisance in my own House.
As I live & am a man, this is an unexaggerated Tale—my Dreams
became the substances of my Life.'

1. To whom does 'such men' in line 49 refer?
2. Lines 41–48 are puzzling, but their meaning can be worked
out. Attempt a paraphrase of these lines. (N.B. Coleridge may
have coined the word 'entempesting' in line 45. It is given in the

dictionary as being formed on the analogy of 'engulf', 'enmesh', etc.)

3. What is there in the poem more than we learn from the prose quotations from letters to Southey and Poole?

4. Wordsworth and Coleridge had been interested in what is known as Pantheism.* What evidence is there in the first section of this poem to indicate an interest in it on Coleridge's part and a deviation from Orthodox Christian practice?

5. This is clearly an honest poem. What evidence is there in section 3 of reticence, and what evidence of inner conflict?

6. Of the technical achievement of this poem, would you say that 'contrived', 'spontaneous' or 'polished' is the best single epithet? Coleridge, who often depreciated his poems, calls the verse 'doggrels'. Was he right? What is doggerel? Give an example of doggerel written by anyone except Coleridge.

7. Give examples from this poem of archaism, and inversion of the natural word-order.

8. Coleridge wonders why he is being visited with the punishment of nightmares when he feels no sense of sin. We know that his distress was caused by his taking the opium he needed to kill pain, but he was something of a pioneer as an opium-eater and its effects were not fully known in 1803. If Coleridge had known of them, and of the distressing symptoms caused by the attempt to give up the drug, what difference would it have made to the poem? Could the poem now be used as propaganda against drug-addiction?

9. Are you satisfied with the poem as it is, or do you feel tempted to find out more about Coleridge by reading his letters and journals? What, for instance, do you make of the final couplet, which comes as something of a surprise?

* The view that the Deity is inherent in all things, and especially in animate nature.

Part III

47. ANONYMOUS: *Llywarch the Old* [Translated from the Welsh by Anthony Conran]

[In the second sequence from the Llywarch Hen cycle. Llywarch is left alone, his sons—even Llawr and Gwên, the last of them—are all dead because of his proud taunting of them, and the old man, bent over a crooked stick, mourns his isolation and despair.]

Ere my back was bent, I was ready with words:
My prowess was praised.
Men of Argoed ever upheld me.

Ere my back was bent, I was bold,
Was welcomed in the beer-hall   5
Of Powys, paradise of Welshmen.

Ere my back was bent, I was brilliant.
My spear was the first to strike.
A hunchback now, I am heavy and wretched.

Wooden crook, it is autumn.   10
Bracken red, stubble sere.
I've surrendered all I love.

Wooden crook, it is winter.
Men shout gaily over the drink.
At my bedside, no one greets me.   15

Wooden crook, it is springtime.
Cuckoos hid, clear their grieving.
I'm disregarded by a girl.

Wooden crook, it is maytime.
Red the furrow, shoots are curled.   20
For me to gaze at your beak is woe!

Wooden crook, familiar branch,
Prop an old man full of longing—
Llywarch, the steadfast talker!

Wooden crook, hard branch,   25
God my help will welcome me—
Good stick, my true companion!

Wooden crook, be kind—
Even better prop me up,
Llywarch, the long loquacious!   30

Old age is mocking me
From my hair to my teeth
And the knob that youth loves.

Old age is mocking me
From my hair to my teeth   35
And the knob women love.

Boisterous wind. White skirts
To the trees. Stag brave, bleak hill.
The old man frail. Slow he rises.

This leaf, chased here and there by the wind,   40
    Its destiny's drear.
  It is old; it was born this year.

What I loved as a lad is hateful to me—
    A girl, a stranger, a spry horse.
  No indeed they do not suit me.   45

The four chief things I hated
Have come now all at once:
Coughing and old age, sickness and sorrow.

I am old, and alone, and shapeless with cold.
    My bed was once splendid   50
  I'm doubled in three, and wretched.

I am old, bent in three, I am fickle and reckless,
    I'm a fool, and uncouth.
  They that once loved me, do not now.

Not a girl loves me, no one comes near me,   55
    I cannot seek them.
    O for death, to end me!

There comes to me neither sleep nor mirth
Now that Llawr and Gwên are dead.
I'm but a querulous corpse, being old.   60

Wretched the fortune doled out to Llywarch
    The night he was born:
    Tired grief, and an age to mourn.

48. Compare (a) and (b)

(a) ANONYMOUS: *The Unquiet Grave*

    Cold blows the wind tonight, sweetheart,
    Cold are the drops of rain.
    The very first love that ever I had
    In greenwood he was slain.

    I'll do as much for my true love   5
    As any young woman may.
    I'll sit and mourn above his grave
    A twelvemonth and a day.

    A twelvemonth and a day being up
    The ghost began to speak.   10
    Why sit you here by my graveside
    And will not let me sleep?

    O think upon the garden, love,
    Where you and I did walk.
    The fairest flower that blossomed there   15
    Is withered on the stalk.

    The stalk will bear no leaves, sweetheart,
    The flowers will never return,
    And my true love is dead, is dead,
    And I do nought but mourn.   20

    What is it that you want of me
    And will not let me sleep?

Your salten tears they trickle down
And wet my winding sheet.

What is it that I want of thee,   25
O what of thee in thy grave?
A kiss from off thy clay cold lips,
And that is all I crave.

Now if you were not true in word
As now I know you be   30
I'd tear you as the withered leaves
Are torn from off the tree.

Now I have mourned upon his grave
A twelve month and a day,
I'll set my sail before the wind   35
To waft me far away.

Cold are my lips in death, sweetheart,
My breath is earthly strong.
If you do touch my clay cold lips
Your time will not be long.   40

Cold though your lips in death, sweetheart,
One kiss is all I crave.
I care not, if I kiss but thee,
That I should share thy grave.

(b) THOMAS HARDY: '*Ah, are you digging on my grave?*'

'Ah, are you digging on my grave,
   My loved one?—planting rue?'
—'No: yesterday he went to wed
One of the brightest wealth has bred.
"It cannot hurt her now," he said,   5
   "That I should not be true." '

'Then who is digging on my grave?
   My nearest dearest kin?'
—'Ah, no: they sit and think, "What use!
What good will planting flowers produce?   10
No tendance of her mound can loose
   Her spirit from Death's gin." '

'But some one digs upon my grave?
    My enemy?—prodding sly?'
—'Nay: when she heard you had passed the Gate   15
That shuts on all flesh soon or late,
She thought you no more worth her hate,
    And cares not where you lie.'

'Then, who is digging on my grave?
    Say—since I have not guessed!'   20
—'O it is I, my mistress dear,
Your little dog, who still lives near,
And much I hope my movements here
    Have not disturbed your rest?'

'Ah, yes! *You* dig upon my grave . . .   25
    Why flashed it not on me
That one true heart was left behind!
What feeling do we ever find
To equal among human kind
    A dog's fidelity!'   30

'Mistress, I dug upon your grave
    To bury a bone, in case
I should be hungry near this spot
When passing on my daily trot.
I am sorry, but I quite forgot   35
    It was your resting-place.'

49. Compare (a) and (b)

(a) MATTHEW ARNOLD: *The Last Word*

    Creep into thy narrow bed,
    Creep, and let no more be said!
    Vain thy onset! all stands fast.
    Thou thyself must break at last.

    Let the long contention cease!   5
    Geese are swans, and swans are geese.

Let them have it how they will!
Thou art tired; best be still.

They out-talk'd thee, hiss'd thee, tore thee?
Better men fared thus before thee;   10
Fired their ringing shot and pass'd,
Hotly charged—and sank at last.

Charge once more, then, and be dumb!
Let the victors, when they come,
When the forts of folly fall,   15
Find thy body by the wall!

(b) JOHN DRYDEN: *Momus to Diana, Mars and Venus*

All, all of a piece throughout:
    Thy chase had a beast in view;
Thy wars brought nothing about;
    Thy lovers were all untrue.
'Tis well an old age is out,   5
    And time to begin a new.

[*The Secular Monk*, performed in 1700, celebrated the end of the
century. It continued in satirical form Dryden's condemnation
of the age he lived in. Momus was the God of mockery.]

50. Compare (a), (b) and (c)

(a) MATTHEW ARNOLD: *Shakespeare*

Others abide our question. Thou art free
We ask and ask—Thou smilest and art still,
Out-topping knowledge. For the loftiest hill,
Who to the stars uncrowns his majesty,

Planting his steadfast footsteps in the sea,   5
Making the heaven of heavens his dwelling-place,
Spares but the cloudy border of his base
To the foil'd searching of mortality;

And thou, who didst the stars and sunbeams know,
Self-school'd, self-scann'd, self-honour'd, self-secure,   10
Didst tread on earth unguess'd at.—Better so!

All pains the immortal spirit must endure,
All weakness which impairs, all griefs which bow,
Find their sole speech in that victorious brow.

(b) JOHN MILTON: *An Epitaph on the admirable dramatic poet W. Shakespeare.* 1630

What needs my Shakespeare for his honour'd bones,
The labour of an age in pilèd stones?
Or that his hallow'd reliques should be hid
Under a star-y-pointing pyramid?
Dear son of memory, great heir of fame,   5
What need'st thou such weak witness of thy name?
Thou in our wonder and astonishment
Hast built thyself a live-long monument.
For whilst to the shame of slow-endeavouring art
The easy numbers flow, and that each heart   10
Hath from the leaves of thy unvalued book
Those Delphic lines with deep impression took,
Then thou our fancy of itself bereaving,
Dost make us marble with too much conceiving;
And so sepúlchred in such pomp dost lie,   15
That kings for such a tomb would wish to die.

(c) A. C. SWINBURNE: *William Shakespeare*

Not if men's tongues and angels' all in one
    Spake, might the word be said that might speak
            Thee.
    Streams, winds, woods, flowers, fields, mountains,
            yea, the sea,
What power is in them all to praise the sun?
His praise is this,—he can be praised of none.   5
    Man, woman, child, praise God for him; but he
    Exults not to be worshipped, but to be.
He is; and, being, beholds his work well done.

All joy, all glory, all sorrow, all strength, all mirth,
Are his: without him, day were night on earth.   10
   Time knows not his from time's own period.
All lutes, all harps, all viols, all flutes, all lyres,
Fall dumb before him ere one string suspires.
   All stars are angels; but the sun is God.

51. THOMAS ASHE: *Meet we no Angels, Pansie?*

Came, on a Sabbath noon, my sweet,
   In white, to find her lover;
The grass grew proud beneath her feet,
   The green elm-leaves above her:—
     Meet we no angels, Pansie?   5

She said, 'We meet no angels now';
   And soft lights stream'd upon her;
And with white hand she touch'd a bough;
   She did it that great honour:—
     What! meet no angels, Pansie?   10

O sweet brown hat, brown hair, brown eyes,
   Down-dropp'd brown eyes, so tender!
Then what said I? Gallant replies
   Seem flattery, and offend her:—
     But—meet no angels, Pansie?   15

52. KENNETH H. ASHLEY: *Goods Train at Night*

The station is empty and desolate;
   A sick lamp wanly glows;
Slowly puffs a goods engine,
   Slow yet alive with great energy;
Drawing rumbling truck   5
   After rumbling, rumbling truck;
Big, half-seen, insensate.
   Yet each as it jolts through the glow

Responds to the questioning light
Humbly revealing   10
Diverse personality:
'Neal & Co.'; 'John Bugsworth'; 'Norland
    Colleries Limited';
'Jolly & Sons'; 'Jolly & Sons'; 'Jolly &
    Sons';
Thrice repeated, percussive, insistent—
Each wet wall-side successively announcing   15
Names: badges and symbols of men,
Of men in their intricate trafficking—
But there quickens a deeper emotion,
Roused by the iterant names,
Beyond the mere intricate commerce,   20
The infinite wonder of life.
Effort and hope and love, the heart's desire,
Leap in the womb of the brain
As the trucks clang their way through the night
Slides by the guard's van at the last,   25
With a last definite clatter of steel upon steel
And a glitter of ruby-red light.

So: silence recaptures the station;
The damp steam eddies out;
The drizzle weaves a silver pattern,   30
An endless shining silver pattern,
A silver wood in the lamplight.
And I find myself full of a grief—
A dull little grief for humanity.

53. Compare (a) and (b)

(a) THOMAS HAYNES BAYLY: *Remember Me*

Remember me when I am gone,
I still would claim the thoughts of *one*,
And Anna thou wilt ever be
The *one* I wish to think of me.
When winds are fair, and sails are set,   5

I only ask one heart's regret;
And oh, how blest should I discern
One welcome smile when I return.

I only ask where'er I rove,
A few dear friends, and one dear love;   10
My muse has fame enough if one
For my sake listens to its tone.
In fields of war one potent charm
Shall warm my heart and nerve my arm;
In conquest I shall only need   15
One cheering voice to praise the deed.

Enjoyment loses half its worth
Till one is near to share my mirth;
And sorrow's pang is less severe
If *one* consoling form is near.   20
Remember me when I am gone,
I still would claim the thoughts of one.
And Anna, thou wilt ever be
The one I wish to think of me.

(b) JOHN DONNE: *His Picture*

Here take my Picture, though I bid farewell;
Thine, in my heart, where my soule dwels, shall dwell.
'Tis like me now, but I dead, 'twill be more
When wee are shadowes both, then 'twas before.
When weather-beaten I come backe; my hand,   5
Perchance with rude oares torne, or Sun beams tann'd,
My face and brest of haircloth, and my head
With cares rash sodaine hoarinesse o'rspread,
My body's a sack of bones, broken within,
And powders blew staines scatter'd on my skinne;   10
If rivall fooles taxe thee to'have lov'd a man,
So foule, and course, as, Oh, I may seeme than,
This shall say what I was: and thou shalt say,
Doe his hurts reach mee? doth my worth decay?
Or doe they reach his judging minde, that hee   15
Should like'and love lesse, what hee did love to see?

That which in him was faire and delicate,
Was but the milke, which in loves childish state
Did nurse it: who now is growne strong enough
To feed on that, which to'disus'd tasts seemes tough.   20

---

54. S. T. COLERIDGE: *Sonnet*

To the River Otter

Dear native brook! wild streamlet of the West!
　How many various-fated years have past,
　　What happy, and what mournful hours, since last
I skimmed the smooth thin stone along thy breast,
Numbering its light leaps! yet so deep imprest   5
Sink the sweet scenes of childhood, that mine eyes
　I never shut amid the sunny ray,
But straight with all their tints thy waters rise,
　Thy crossing plank, thy marge with willows grey,
And bedded sand that, veined with various dyes,   10
Gleamed through thy bright transparence! On my way,
　Visions of childhood! oft have ye beguiled
Lone manhood's cares, yet waking fondest sighs:
　Ah! that once more I were a careless child!

---

55. KEITH DOUGLAS: *Egypt*

　　Aniseed has a sinful taste:
　　at your elbow a woman's voice
　　like, I imagine, the voice of ghosts,
　　demanding food. She has no grace

　　but, diseased and blind of an eye   5
　　and heavy with habitual dolour,
　　listlessly finds you and I
　　and the table are the same colour.

　　The music, the harsh talk, the fine
　　clash of the drinkseller's tray,   10

are the same to her, as her own whine;
she knows no variety.

And in fifteen years of living
found nothing different from death
but the difference of moving   15
and the nuisance of breath.

A disguise of ordure can't hide
her beauty, succumbing in a cloud
of disease, disease, apathy. My God,
the king of this country must be proud.   20

Egypt, 1942

56. ELENA FEARN: *Snow-man and Snow-woman*

They had not planned to meet, it was sheer luck,
That encounter where they stood
Hobbled on their snow legs, and their snow eyes
Ready to run, and blurred.

There was nothing to speak of but the weather,   5
And nothing but a pleasant grin to give—
Although that was enough, and showed their pride
In knowing it genius to be snow and live.

Each bore within a red-hot coal to melt them,
Though outside as hard as any stone;   10
Therefore his clumsy courtesy and these stares
For the occasion—this, the only one.

For next time they meet, another year
Perhaps, still strange, still lucky,
He'll be a different man and she another woman   15
Under their enduring symmetry.

57. Compare (a) and (b)

(a) THOMAS HOOD: *I Remember, I Remember*

I

> I remember, I remember,
> The house where I was born,
> The little window where the sun
> Came peeping in at morn;
> He never came a wink too soon,   5
> Nor brought too long a day,
> But now, I often wish the night
> Had borne my breath away!

II

> I remember, I remember,
> The roses, red and white,   10
> The vi'lets, and the lily-cups,
> Those flowers made of light!
> The lilacs where the robin built,
> And where my brother set
> The laburnum on his birthday,—   15
> The tree is living yet!

III

> I remember, I remember,
> Where I was used to swing,
> And thought the air must rush as fresh
> To swallows on the wing;   20
> My spirit flew in feathers then,
> That is so heavy now,
> And summer pools could hardly cool
> The fever on my brow!

IV

> I remember, I remember,   25
> The fir trees dark and high;
> I used to think their slender tops
> Were close against the sky:
> It was a childish ignorance,
> But now 'tis little joy   30
> To know I'm farther off from heav'n
> Than when I was a boy.

(b) CHARLES LAMB: *The Old Familiar Faces*

Where are they gone, the old familiar faces?

I had a mother, but she died, and left me,
Died prematurely in a day of horrors—
All, all are gone, the old familiar faces.

I have had playmates, I have had companions,   5
In my days of childhood, in my joyful school-days—
All, all are gone, the old familiar faces.

I have been laughing, I have been carousing,
Drinking late, sitting late, with my bosom cronies—
All, all are gone, the old familiar faces.   10

I loved a love once, fairest among women.
Closed are her doors on me, I must not see her—
All, all are gone, the old familiar faces.

I have a friend, a kinder friend has no man.
Like an ingrate, I left my friend abruptly;   15
Left him, to muse on the old familiar faces.

Ghost-like, I paced round the haunts of my childhood.
Earth seem'd a desert I was bound to traverse,
Seeking to find the old familiar faces.

Friend of my bosom, thou more than a brother!   20
Why wert not thou born in my father's dwelling?
So might we talk of the old familiar faces.

For some they have died, and some they have left me,
And some are taken from me; all are departed;
All, all are gone, the old familiar faces.   25

58. GERARD MANLEY HOPKINS: *I Wake and Feel the Fell of Dark*

> I wake and feel the fell of dark, not day.
> What hours, O what black hoürs we have spent
> This night! what sights you, heart, saw; ways you went!
> And more must, in yet longer light's delay.
>   With witness I speak this. But where I say   5
> Hours I mean years, mean life. And my lament
> It cries countless, cries like dead letters sent
> To dearest him that lives alas! away.
>
> I am gall, I am heartburn. God's most deep decree
> Bitter would have me taste: my taste was me;   10
> Bones built in me, flesh filled, blood brimmed the curse
>   Selfyeast of spirit a dull dough sours. I see
> The lost are like this, and their scourge to be
> As I am mine, their sweating selves; but worse.

59. Compare (a) and (b)

(a) JOHN KEATS: Stanzas XIV, XV, XVI from *Isabella*

> With her two brothers this fair lady dwelt,
>   Enriched from ancestral merchandise,
> And for them many a weary hand did swelt
>   In torched mines and noisy factories,
> And many once proud-quiver'd loins did melt   5
>   In blood from stinging whip;—with hollow eyes,
> Many all day in dazzling river stood,
> To take the rich-ored driftings of the flood.
>
> XV
>
> For them the Ceylon diver held his breath,
>   And went all naked to the hungry shark;   10
> For them his ears gush'd blood; for them in death.
>   The seal on the cold ice with piteous bark

Lay full of darts; for them alone did seethe
A thousand men in troubles wide and dark:
Half-ignorant, they turn'd an easy wheel,   15
That set sharp racks at work, to pinch and peel.

XVI

Why were they proud? Because their marble founts
Gush'd with more pride than do a wretch's tears?—
Why were they proud? Because fair orange-mounts
Were of more soft ascent than lazar stairs?—   20
Why were they proud? Because red-lin'd accounts
Were richer than the songs of Grecian years?—
Why were they proud? again we ask aloud,
Why in the name of Glory were they proud?

(b) WILFRED OWEN: *Miners*

There was a whispering in my hearth,
    A sigh of the coal,
Grown wistful of a former earth
    It might recall.

I listened for a tale of leaves   5
    And smothered ferns;
Frond-forests; and the low, sly lives
    Before the fawns.

My fire might show steam-phantoms simmer
    From Time's old cauldron,   10
Before the birds made nests in summer,
    Or men had children.

But the coals were murmuring of their mine,
    And moans down there
Of boys that slept wry sleep, and men   15
    Writhing for air.

And I saw white bones in the cinder-shard.
    Bones without number;
For many hearts with coal are charred
    And few remember.   20

I thought of some who worked dark pits
    Of war, and died
Digging the rock where Death reputes
    Peace lies indeed.

Comforted years will sit soft-chaired   25
    In rooms of amber;
The years will stretch their hands, well-cheered
    By our lives' ember.

The centuries will burn rich loads
    With which we groaned,   30
Whose warmth shall lull their dreaming lids
    While songs are crooned.
But they will not dream of us poor lads
    Lost in the ground.

60. ALUN LEWIS: *In Hospital: Poona* (I)

Last night I did not fight for sleep
But lay awake from midnight while the world
Turned its slow features to the moving deep
Of darkness, till I knew that you were furled,

Beloved, in the same dark watch as I.   5
And sixty degrees of longitude beside
Vanished as though a swan in ecstasy
Had spanned the distance from your sleeping side.

And like to swan or moon the whole of Wales
Glided within the parish of my care: 10
I saw the green tide leap on Cardigan,
Your red yacht riding like a legend there,

And the great mountains, Dafydd and Llewelyn,
Plynlimmon, Cader Idris and Eryri
Threshing the darkness back from head and fin,   15
And also the small nameless mining valley

M   .

Whose slopes are scratched with streets and sprawling graves
Dark in the lap of firwoods and great boulders
Where you lay waiting, listening to the waves—
My hot hands touched your white despondent shoulders   20

—And then ten thousand miles of daylight grew
Between us, and I heard the wild daws crake
In India's starving throat; whereat I knew
That Time upon the heart can break
But love survives the venom of the snake.   25

61. ROGER L'ESTRANGE: *Mr Le Strange his Verses in the Prison at Linn*

Beat on, proud billows; Boreas, blow;
    Swell, curled waves, high as Jove's roof;
Your incivility shall know
    That innocence is tempest-proof:
Though surly Nereus roar, my thoughts are calm;   5
Then strike, affliction, for thy wounds are balm.

That which the world recalls a jail,
    A private closet is to me,
Whilst a good conscience is my bail,
    And innocence my liberty: 10
Locks, bars, walls, loneliness, together met,
Make me no prisoner, but an anchoret.

I, while I wished to be retired,
    Into this private room was turned,
As if their wisdoms had conspired   15
    A salamander should be burned;
Or like those sophies that would drown a fish,
I am constrained to suffer what I wish.

So he, that struck at Jason's life
    Thinking to make his purpose sure,   20
By a malicious friendly knife
    Did only wound him to a cure:
Malice, I see, wants wit, for what it meant,
Mischief, oft times proves favour in the event.

These manacles upon mine arm   25
   I as my sweetheart's favours wear;
And then to keep mine ankles warm
   I have some iron shackles there.
Contentment cannot smart, stoics we see
Make torments easy by their apathy.   30

Here sin for want of food doth starve
   Where tempting objects are not seen;
And these strong walls do only serve
   To keep vice out, and keep me in:
Malice of late grows charitable sure,   35
I'm not committed, but I'm kept secure.

When once my prince affliction hath,
   Prosperity doth treason seem;
And then to smooth so rough a path
   I can learn patience e'en from him: 40
Now not to suffer shows no loyal heart,
When kings want ease, subjects must learn to smart.

What though I cannot see my king
   Either in his person or his coin;
Yet contemplation is a thing   45
   Will render what I have not, mine:
My king from me what adamant can part
Whom I do wear engraven in my heart.

My soul's as free as the ambient air,
   Although my baser part's immured,   50
While loyal thoughts do still repair
   To accompany my solitude:
And though rebellion do my body bind
My king can only captivate my mind.

Have you beheld the nightingale,   55
   A pilgrim turned into a cage,
How still she tells her wonted tale
   In this her private hermitage?

E'en here her chanting melody doth prove
That all her bars are trees, her cage a grove.   60

I am the bird whom they combine
  Thus to deprive of liberty;
And though they do my corpse confine,
  Yet, maugre hate, my soul is free:
And though immured, yet here I'll chirp and sing,   65
Disgrace to rebels, glory to my King.

62. EDWIN MUIR: *Suburban Dream*

Walking the suburbs in the afternoon
In summer when the idle doors stand open
  And the air flows through the rooms
  Fanning the curtain hems,

You wander through a cool elysium   5
Of women, schoolgirls, children, garden talks.
  With a schoolboy here and there
  Coming his history book.

The men are all away in offices,
Committee-rooms, laboratories, banks,   10
  Or pushing cotton goods
  In Wick or Ilfracombe.

The massed unanimous absence liberates
The light keys of the piano and sets free
  Chopin and everlasting youth,   15
  Now, with the masters gone.

And all things turn to images of peace,
The boys curled over his book, the young girl poised
  On the path as if beguiled
  By the silence of a wood.   20

It is a child's dream of a grown-up world.
But soon the brazen evening clocks will bring
  The tramp of feet and brisk
  Fanfare of motor horns
  And the masters come.   25

63. J. ENOCH POWELL: *Alexander*

>Fairest of mortal men, though scarred
>From foot to head with battle-rage,
>Youngest in heart, though steely hard
>And wiser than the sage.

>Well did the astonished Greeks acclaim 5
>The prince and saviour of mankind
>And hallow temples in the name
>Of thy all-conquering mind;

>And rightly Ammon's oracle
>In thee the son of Zeus perceived, 10
>Because the long-sought miracle
>Thy birth divine achieved:

>Only a god could bring to light
>The incarnate truth that sets men free—
>That beauty there is none but might 15
>Nor youth but victory

64. HENRY REED: *Outside and In*

>Suddenly I knew that you were outside the house.
>The trees went silent you were prowling among,
>The twig gave warning, snapped in the evening air,
>And all the birds in the garden finished singing.
>What have you come for? Have you come in peace? 5
>Or have you come to blackmail, or just to know?

>And after sunset must I be made to watch
>The lawn and the lane, from the bed drawn to the window,
>The winking glass on top of the garden wall,
>The shadows relaxing and stiffening under the moon? 10
>I am alone, but look, I have opened the doors,
>And the house is filling with cold, the winds blow in.

A house so vulnerable and divided, with
A mutiny already inside its walls,
Cannot withstand a siege. I have opened the doors   15
In sign of surrender. The house is filling with cold.
Why will you stay out there? I am ready to answer.
The doors are open. Why will you not come in?

65. J. M. RUSSELL: *Burma II*

I remember Harley well. It happened when
We'd swept a path across the ridge,
Insane with lust for killing. Then
  We stopped to check our men,
To count our crazy losses on that bridge   5
  Of steel and bone.
  And suddenly a hidden Jap
Lept up and bolted. And a thrown
Grenade dropped at our feet. The slap
Of fear destroyed our new shown   10
  Courage, and Harley stood alone.
  He lost an arm.
  He stood there, numb with pain
And bitter calm
  With hate. And then the charm   15
Of stupefaction passed. His brain
Flamed through his eyes. His good hand
Snatched a Tommy gun in fury, and
  He dashed away. The sand
Reproached us with a spreading stain.   20

Harley returned, mad-light and satisfied,
Flushed more terribly than the crimson he had bled.
He dropped his gun, held out his hand, and cried:
'There's the lousy bastard that got my arm, and died.'

And he threw at my feet a head.   25

66. C. H. SISSON: *Moriturus*

The carcase that awaits the undertaker
But will not give up its small voice lies
Hollow and grim upon the bed.
What stirs in it is hardly life but a morosity
Which when this skipped as a child was already
    under the lids   5
Rebellious and parting from the flesh.

What drunken fury in adolescence pretended
Merely to possess the flesh and drove onwards
The blind soul to issue in the lap of Venus?

The hope of fatherhood, watching the babe sucking   10
(Ah, he will grow, hurled headlong into the tomb!)
Gives way to a tenderness spilt into amnesia.

The last chat of corruption reasonable as a syllogism
The image of God is clear, his love wordless
Untie my ligaments, let my bones disperse.   15

67. EDMUND SPENSER: *Sonnet XXVIII* from *Absoretti*

The laurell leafe, which you this day doe weare,
Gives me great hope of your relenting mynd;
For since it is the badge which I doe beare,
Ye, bearing it, doe seeme to me inclind:
The powre thereof, which ofte in me I find,   5
Let it lykewise your gentle brest inspire
With sweet infusion, and put you in mind
Of that proud mayd, whom now those leaves attyre:
Proud Daphne, scorning Phœbus lovely fyre,
On the Thessalian shore from him did flie;   10
For which the gods, in theyr revengefull yre,
Did her transforme into a laurell tree.
   Then fly no more, fayre love, from Phebus chace,
   But in your brest his leafe and love embrace.

68. TRUMBULL STICKNEY: *Six o'clock*

Now burst above the city's cold twilight
The piercing whistles and the tower-clocks:
For day is done. Along the frozen docks
The workmen set their ragged shirts aright.
Thro' factory doors a stream of dingy light   5
Follows the scrimmage as it quickly flocks
To hut and home among the snow's gray blocks.—
I love you, human labourers. Good-night!
Good-night to all the blackened arms that ache!
Good-night to every sick and sweated brow,   10
To the poor girl that strength and love forsake,
To the poor boy who can no more! I vow
The victim soon shall shudder at the stake
And fall in blood: we bring him even now.

69. ANDREW YOUNG: *On the Hillside*

What causes the surprise
That greets me here under the piecemeal skies
Of this thick-wooded scar?
Is it the look that the familiar
Keeps as of something strange   5
When so much else is constant but to change?
No, it's the thought that this white sun that cleaves
A silvery passage through the leaves
Is the same sun that cleft them
A week ago, as though I never left them   10
And never went in the sad interval
To my friend's funeral,
Though crossing the churchyard to-day I shivered
To see how fast on a fresh grave the flowers had withered.

Index of Authors, Titles and First Lines